Toni Erickson has poured a lifetime of top expertise into this valuable addition to the couples therapy genre. Her compassion, wisdom, and experience are evident on every page of this comprehensive, don't-raise-children-without-this guidebook. It is so challenging to keep a marriage thriving with the challenges of raising a family. This advice is practical and actionable. She offers creative suggestions for keeping love alive and comprehensive help for handling common problems. I wish I'd had this knowledge when I raised my family!

Tommi Wolfe
CEO, The Startup Expert
www.Top6BusinessCoach.com

Toni Erickson's book, Keeping Romance Alive After Children Arrive, *is a wonderful book, full of her experience and wisdom. It is filled with tools that couples can use to work on their own to improve and/or heal their marriage, especially during the difficult challenges that life throws us. Those couples having a new baby or who already have children will find it most valuable. I recommend it without hesitation!*

John Rifkin, PhD, is the author of *The Healing Power of Anger*, which was nominated for the William James Book Award of the American Psychological Association.

As a long-time family mediator, I've met many couples who have lost their loving feelings early in the marriage. Not knowing how to reclaim them, they see divorce as the only path out of the quagmire of conflict or lack of connection that increased family pressures bring. By following the wisdom of Toni Erickson, "The Marriage Mentor," spouses can learn new skills and approaches to keeping their love fresh and intact throughout the many trials and tribulations of family life. Thus they can avoid the pain and loss of their dreams and mates that divorce brings. Keeping Romance Alive After Children Arrive *is a guide to successful coupling and relationship sustenance that is easy to read and put into practice.*

Christine A. Coates, J.D., is co–author of *Learning from Divorce: How to Take Responsibility, Stop the Blame and Move On.*

I was excited when Toni, who is my friend as well as a fellow coach and therapist, called and asked if I would be willing to read her new book, giving it a recommendation if I "felt it was worthy." I was honored, and I knew it would be worthy of a heartfelt, positive recommendation before I read the first word! I've known Toni for more than 14 years, now, both personally and professionally. She is loving, caring, dedicated, talented—and most of all, effective. Her new book is called Keeping Romance Alive After Children Arrive. *If that in any way describes you now, or will describe you in the future, do yourself a big favor and buy a copy of this book. I know you will be richly rewarded.*

Jack Bergstrom / Coach, Speaker, Author
Former assistant to Tony Robbins and veteran of more than 21,000 one–on–one coaching sessions
www.jackbergstrom.com

Keeping Romance Alive After Children Arrive

How to Thrive in a Loving and Passionate Marriage While Raising a Happy Family

Toni Erickson, MSW, LCSW
"The Marriage Mentor"

DLD Books

ISBN: 1544610246

ISBN13: 978-1544610245

**Dedicated to my husband,
my wonderful children,
their beautiful families,
and those yet to come.**

I Will Never Leave You

When your sky is cold and lonely
and your heart is filled with fear,
I will wrap my arms around you.
Know that I am here.

And I will keep you safe and sound
Through the darkness that surrounds.

I will never leave you, nor forsake you.
Know that I am with you. You will never be alone.

When your way is bright and glowing
and your soul knows no despair,
Can you hear me singing with you?
In your triumph I will share.

For I am watching over you,
And I rejoice in all you do.

I will never leave you, nor forsake you.
Know that I am with you. You will never be alone.

So remember, never doubt this.
Hold it tightly to your heart.

I'm forever, always with you.
I will be right where you are.

I will never leave you, nor forsake you.
Know that I am with you. You will never be alone.

* * * * *

This is a hauntingly beautiful song I found on YouTube.
I invite you to listen to it.
Though it may be intended to mean
that God will never leave us,
I also dedicate these sentiments to my husband and family.
May we all be so committed to our partners and families
as well as knowing He will never leave us.

The song was written by Jay Stocker
for Scripture Lullabies/BreakAway Music, Inc.
© 2009 BreakAway Music, Inc.
www.Scripture-lullabies.com
Permission was graciously granted by Scripture Lullabies
to use these words.

Acknowledgments

First of all, I am immensely grateful for my wonderful husband, Eric Erickson, whose love and caring have made me such a happy, contented, and joy-filled person. His deep devotion and commitment to our marriage and to my family have inspired my life in many ways. He has blessed me dearly with his inspiration, friendship, and ever–abiding encouragement. I am very appreciative for his attentive and loving support of my role as wife and mother, in my work as a therapist, and in my numerous and varied activities, hobbies, and interests, especially in writing this book.

We met one another later in life after both of us had our children and were divorced from our previous spouses. People seem amazed that we get along so well with our former mates. However, it was a decision all of us made a long time ago to do what was best for our children. I know it has served everyone well. Between us, we have six outstanding children and an ever–expanding family. I am so thankful for their love, reassurance, championing, and affirmation. Their life examples have been exceptional. Constant reinforcement from them has assured me that what I write might provide service, not only to them but to others, as well.

I feel deeply indebted to my sister, Camille Lamoreaux King, who has always been an example of inspiration, love, and support to me. My parents were also great influences in my life. Additionally, many colleagues, friends, and extended family have afforded encouragement and reinforcement, for which I am most appreciative.

I am also indebted to my therapy and coaching clients over the past 30 years, for they have shared their joys and challenges and have provided me an opportunity to be of assistance to them. It is heartwarming that many have communicated their stories of how working together has improved their lives. I have learned much from them, and I'm so pleased they have allowed me into their hearts, minds, and relationships.

Several years ago, I attending a writing class facilitated by Ed Lowe at the Boulder First Presbyterian Church. He inspired my creative juices and propelled me to write stories about my life and my family. I then took a class from Donna Kozik, facilitator of "Write a Book in a Weekend" (frankly, it has taken me much longer than a weekend), who helped me get serious about my writing and got me focused on this book. I thank her, as well as the many writing buddies in our class.

I particularly want to express appreciation to my wonderful primary editor and writing mentor, John Kadlecek, for his guidance in refining and polishing my work. His expertise, wisdom, and encouragement have meant the world to me. I could not have done this without him.

Email: JohnKadlecek@me.com

Website: www. JohnKadlecek.com

Additionally, I want to extend sincere thanks to David and Leonore Dvorkin of DLD Books for final proofing, editing, formatting, and designing. I have been very pleased with their work.

Email: david@dvorkin.com

Website: www.dldbooks.com

Finally, I am especially grateful to God for the love, inspiration, and blessings I have received throughout my life. My gratitude is immeasurable.

Toni

Table of Contents

Chapter X
Strategies, Solutions, and Exercises
for Enhancing Your Marriage While Parenting.................. 225

INTRODUCTION

Getting married is perhaps the most significant decision two people will ever make in their entire lives. The second most important decision or event is having a child.

If you are expectant parents, I hope you are looking forward with great anticipation to the arrival of your little one. Most couples who embark upon this journey have no idea what is to come. If you have already had a baby, you are at least aware of some of the snags and snares involved in maintaining a close and loving marriage. At the same time, you are also cognizant of the beautiful gift a child is to your family.

Those couples who have abiding love, mutual respect, and deep friendship will undoubtedly experience a happy life together; and if they decide to have children, they will have the opportunity to provide a loving and secure environment for their family and literally turn a house, apartment, or hovel into a home. Sometimes it may take guidance, a pathway, and development of skills, but with enough practice and commitment, outstanding marriages and joyful families can become a reality.

For me, having and raising my own four children has been the most marvelous experience of my life. I would not trade it for anything. You are embarking upon a glorious adventure if you are expecting your first baby or adding another precious child to your family.

Today many individuals opt not to get married, and even fewer decide to have children. Certainly, people are able to elect not to have babies (unless they make a precarious mistake or are unable to conceive). There is no question that their lives can be full of great and amazing experiences. Obviously, not everyone is cut out to be nor wants to be a parent. But those who intentionally make that choice *may potentially* be missing out on one of the most meaningful occurrences in the world. There is nothing else equal to taking on the awesome responsibility for the life of another human being. And it all starts as a beautiful miracle of nature—the birth of a baby.

The Impact of Children

It is heartening to hear stories from parents whose lives became better after having a baby. To some, it comes naturally and harmoniously and the marriage is more enhanced than ever, even from the very beginning.

On the other side are couples whose lives and marriages are challenged dramatically. Children can have a huge impact upon the quality of marriage. It is certainly a mixture of joy, bliss, and delight, as well as fatigue, frustration, and even feelings of failure. Many couples survive the difficult times and are happy together, while others begin to experience a gradual decline in the amazing love they had in the beginning of their relationship. This change may seem surprising, because most people are very much in love when they get married. Somehow they believe their love will see them through. But it takes much more than love and a ceremony.

In my therapy practice, many clients have come to me struggling with their marital relationships. Upon careful inspection, they have recognized, even many years later, that some of their challenging issues began shortly after having a baby, because they allowed events to negatively affect their partnership. At the time, they were not aware of where the problems began. Discontent, unhappiness, and estrangement resulted, and some even made the choice to divorce. I believe that adeptly handling this period can be a valuable step toward avoiding hopelessness and possibly even divorce.

Keeping love, intimacy, and romance alive, especially during the first several months after having a baby, can be trying. Though not the fault of the child in any way, there are many reasons why this new dynamic can test the best of relationships. The sleepless nights, weary days, overwork, lack of time for each other, and the hardships of maintaining balance are not very conducive to looking sexy at the breakfast table or coming up with romantic surprises for each other.

The other important reason for a possible decline in a couple's intimacy is that often babies and even older children take front and center stage, while the parents' relationship is relegated to the lonely back stage. Though it may be unintentional, mothers are especially prone to giving all their attention to their offspring and little to their husbands. In addition, few couples have sufficient tools to communicate effectively, resolve issues, and mitigate the trials that will surely occur. Lacking such abilities can result in repeated misunderstandings and frequent quarrels. This sets problems into play that may take years to resolve—or may never be resolved.

Why I Wrote This Book

If any of this sounds discouraging, there is good news. With love, dedication, and commitment, plus knowledge, patience, effort, and skill, you can have a vibrant, deeply loving, and healthy marriage and an effective, well–functioning family. That is the purpose of *Keeping Romance Alive After Children Arrive*—to let you know what to expect in your partnership once you embark upon the delightful path of parenting.

Lots of books have been written to prepare you for the practicalities of your pregnancy and how to take care of your baby. However, little has been written about how to manage the emotional, hormonal, and relational changes that will take place. Even less has been revealed about how to keep a close, intimate, and loving connection with your spouse. Although books with tools and skills are available, they are generally not specifically geared toward parents.

When my four children were young, I endured an unexpected divorce. I did the best I could as a parent in those early years. It was enormously demanding at times being a single mother, and I handled things as well as I could. Perhaps the children dealt with it better than I did, for I was an emotional mess for a while. But they turned out beautifully and went on to have wonderful lives and families of their own.

Ten years after the divorce, I entered graduate school to become a Licensed Clinical Social Worker with an emphasis in counseling. During that time, I developed a strong passion for helping couples and families create successful, strong, and loving relationships, something I hadn't experienced during my childhood years or in my first marriage.

Because of events in my own life and the lives of many clients and friends, the ideas for *Keeping Romance Alive After Children Arrive* have been churning around in my mind for a long time. I believed that there was, and is, a tremendous need for a guidebook to help couples remain loving and romantic while raising a family and make the journey of parenthood enriching and joy filled. It is also my goal to provide assistance so they can maintain and strengthen the love and romance that brought them together in the first place, because I know that the fabric of our society needs strong family units and communities in order to survive well.

When they marry, most couples have hopes and dreams of living "happily ever after." This concept doesn't have to be a fairy tale, but it will take conscious and creative effort to make it a reality. Obviously, men and women are different due to their varying life experiences growing up, family influences, and genetic impacts, as well as home, friends, and schooling environments. This means that partners must come to a central place to negotiate and make compromises in order to make things work effectively.

Understanding some of the realities, pitfalls, and trials of marriage—especially when having children—is fundamental to keeping love and romance thriving. That is what this book provides, plus case examples, personal experiences, support, skills, tools, and methods for applying the material for many years to come. Information is powerful, but only application will cause it to be effective.

A successful marriage requires falling in love many times, always with the same person.
—Mignon McLaughlin

Who Keeping Romance Is For

Whether this is your first or your tenth child, the book is full of good advice with examples of realistic and difficult situations, solutions, and exercises to improve your partnership. Though especially directed to married heterosexual couples, it is also suitable for same–sex couples, remarried couples with children, adoptive parents, and those with more than one child. I encourage you to make the necessary adjustments for your particular circumstances, since it is cumbersome to address every possible situation. In addition, I have changed names and situations to protect people's privacy; however, my own family stories are authentic.

How to Use This Book

It is my desire that *Keeping Romance Alive After Children Arrive* will change the way you look at your marriage and will positively influence the ways you and your partner respond together after having a baby and ever after. To make the most of your efforts, I invite you to set aside time to read and learn together no matter how busy, tired, or stressed you become. Take what rings true for you and apply it to your particular situation. Then repeat what works. It's that simple. Loving application is the key.

Though it may be problematic to find moments to study and complete the exercises together, do your best. If you find it impossible, do what you can on your own, and then discuss the ideas with your partner. Your joint commitment to learning for the sake of your relationship will aid you immensely, regardless of whether you study together or separately.

The book explores the topics of love and romance, what to expect when you have a baby, the importance of fathers, communication and conflict resolution skills, intimacy and sex, challenging situations, and many stories describing potential occurrences and how best to deal with them. Please pay special attention to Chapter IX, regarding communication. In that chapter you will find a lot a good information and tools for skill development.

Chapter X has tools and exercises to improve your marriage *at any stage:* how to create your vision, coping with stress, clarifying values and expectations, keys to your lover's heart, the relationship bank account, and much, much more. You may find the three Appendices at the end useful, as well. Appendix A has a list of "How Joyful Partners Treat Each Other," Appendix B provides lots of "Ideas for Keeping Love and Romance Thriving," and Appendix C contains "A Few Parenting Tips."

I strongly suggest that you create your own "Relationship Journal" and record the work you do. At the end of each chapter, you will find "Options for Action." Read through and pick those that resonate for you. You can record your answers, discoveries, and agreements in your journals. As you practice and apply the material, you will have the best chance of creating a loving and rewarding partnership.

Why Read *Keeping Romance Alive*?

Parenting is a beautiful adventure. Even if your marriage is everything you want it to be, you will discover many ideas to enrich and enliven your lives. If your relationship is suffering, I know the book can provide guidance and teach you to resolve your disputes before they become so large that they are overwhelming. But if they do, please also seek counseling, marriage coaching, pastoral assistance, or whatever other resources you can find.

Believe me, I won't be the only one to give you advice on these matters. In fact, you will probably get it by the bushelful, much more than you might ever desire. It will be interesting to see that almost everyone you meet will tell you how to take care of your baby, but not many will share anything about how to keep love and romance thriving. I hope you will benefit greatly from some of the ideas within. My advice is to gather all the information you can from books, articles, parenting groups, etc., because much of it will be indispensable. But in the end, listen to your own heart. No one knows you and your situation as well as you.

Children expect and hope that their families will remain close and loving, so it behooves you to do all you can to create a safe and secure environment. Of special and lasting value is for you to demonstrate how you express love, show affection, resolve disagreements, spend couple time together, and have fun as a family. You are your children's most important role models. No matter how young or how old they are, your job as parents is *never* done. Your task is to make your family feel loved and valued and to create a haven where they feel nurtured, safe, and secure.

Having a child is truly a life–altering experience, one I'm sure will be well worth all the challenges. When that sweet little bundle lies quietly in your arms and looks up at you with his or her big blue or brown eyes and sweet little smile, your heart will melt. So accept this precious gift with open heart and loving arms, for it will be unequaled by anything else in the universe.

I hope this book will make the mountains and valleys easier to navigate and that you will use the material to keep your love shining and the romantic trysts of your relationship abundant.

With dedication and devotion to yourselves and to one another, you can create a stable and enduring marriage, enhance your love, and create the kind of marriage and family you have always dreamed of.

**I wish bountiful happiness and success for you
as a couple and as a family!**

Chapter I
In the Beginning
There Is Love and Romance

Magic is those unexpected surprises and serendipitous moments which seem to appear— sometimes asked for, sometimes not—which delight and amaze us.
—Toni Erickson

Before I get into keeping your love and romance alive after you have a baby and are raising your family, I'd like to start at the beginning with a little background about love.

As many of you were growing up, you dreamed you could find the perfect partner with whom you would fall in love and live with forever in bliss. You believed that life would be full of magic and wonder, and you'd be so perfectly matched that nothing or no one could ever drag you apart. You would focus only on one another, crave being together, enjoy never–ending romantic interludes, and keep passion endlessly flourishing. Though movies, plays, television, and literature probably inspired such magical thinking, some did indeed find true love, while others were sadly disappointed over time or never found an ideal partner.

Wonder and Magic

To those who are fortunate enough to find true love and decide to make one another the center of their world, life may seem extraordinary, incredible, and even magical. Couples are brimming with joy, delight, wonder, and excitement. They may finish each other's sentences, call each other endearing names, and believe that nothing can ever come between them. Life is glorious, energizing, and *very* romantic; their love for one another seems unequaled. Such feelings can cause a person to think about their loved one constantly. They may lose sleep, suffer a loss of appetite, and have trouble concentrating; life becomes distracting in a most delightful way.

If the couple decides to plan a life together, marriage by its very definition involves the merging of two worlds. It includes making a commitment to serve the needs and well–being of one another, letting go of certain individual thoughts and behaviors, learning to get along under stressful circumstances, keeping the magical moments alive, and remaining loyal.

At this point, however, many couples have not thought about what existence together might be like should one of them have a serious illness, lose a job, need to care for an aging parent, or experience any number of unforeseen circumstances. They believe they can get through anything. And certainly they can when there is determination, commitment, caring, and knowledge about how to create a solid and lasting relationship. For some it may not be a simple task, but it is very doable if real desire is present.

Moving from Me to Us

Everyone carries a "backpack" around with both positive and negative incidents derived from years of growing and maturing. Many backpacks contain loving and beautiful experiences, while some carry unhappy and horrible experiences. We bring those events into our relationships. And so it is advantageous to deal with our past in effective ways, so that our present and future can be full of satisfaction, happiness, and peace.

One of the hurdles in maintaining happiness in any new partnership is learning to move from *me* to *us*. Before most couples get married, each individual has usually led a fairly independent life for a while, maybe even for years. Their parents no longer govern their lives, and they may have been away at school or enjoying a career. That independence is likely to have created self–focused habits. Making the shift in thoughts and actions from "life is about *me*" to "life is about *us*" may take time and awareness of what a partnership is all about. However, it is a crucial first step in creating a successful marriage and being able to happily start a family.

Some people make the transition quite easily, while others struggle, wanting to maintain independence and autonomy, or perhaps not even being aware of the need to create *us*. It may be a bit frightening to give up familiar patterns that worked so well in the past to make room for a future with the person with whom you have chosen to share your life. But nothing hastens a decline faster than a huge stressor, an unexpected crisis, or the birth of a baby. At this point, the concept of *us* becomes a real necessity.

What Is Love?

For centuries, people have been attempting to define love. This is difficult, because it means different things to different people; plus, there are so many types of love. Though it is complicated to give an adequate description, at its base are concern, kindness, gentleness, compassion, and caring. Loving individuals are sensitive to others and will never harm or wrongly destroy anything or anyone.

Being "in love" is exhilarating. It is not something that can be planned, demanded, or dictated. It may be invited, but it seems to come in its own way and on its own timing. It just happens. You want to be together, and when you are not, you yearn for your next meeting. Without your lover, your life seems incomplete. Things appear brighter, happier, and more wonderful when you're in love. Your feelings are intense and passionate, and you want to express your affection in intimate ways.

If your love is unselfish, you desire for the one you love to be truly happy, and you will go to extremes to cause it to be so. One of its qualities is selflessness, which is powerful and transforming. It brings relaxation, relief, and uplifting to the heart—like a cushy comforter that warms, nurtures, and blesses. You want to share yourself—your thoughts, feelings, and beliefs—because you feel cherished, safe, and accepted. If you find such love, do not let it go.

Many people are *in love*, but certain others experience *a deep and abiding love* that seems well above the norm. It is amazing, indescribable, euphoric, and lasting. The feeling of love and caring enlivens their hearts and leaves them with a clear sense of serenity, peace, and purpose.

This type of love is unconditional, having no limits or preconditions. Her last thoughts before going to sleep are about him. His desire for her happiness is enormous, and he would do anything for her. She gives him the last piece of birthday cake, and he fixes dinner and puts the kids to bed after her challenging day. She lovingly takes him to physical therapy after a debilitating car accident. He devotedly cares for her for over the years and seeks every cure for her recovery from cancer. Their love is sensitive, creative, grateful, heartfelt, sincere, consistent, dedicated, and more.

Some experience this kind of relationship from the beginning, while others grow into it over time. Either way, it is beautiful, nurturing, and healing. It is a blending of heart, soul, and energy in a way that is as harmonious as the most beautiful piece of music imaginable—the divine sounds of the very universe itself.

If this sounds maudlin, it is not. Those who love like this can weather any storm because they are so close and connected. They desire to work out any difficulties with respect and humility. Both are willing to be open and vulnerable. They truly see one another for who they are, both externally and internally, and are accepting of faults, frailties, and foibles as well as all the treasures which lie within.

It doesn't mean they don't have problems, but their love is based on commitment, openness, sincere communication, loyalty, trust, and mutually shared values and goals. They enjoy a blending of hearts and souls beyond just being friends, companions, sexual lovers, parents, or housemates. The primary goal is *the relationship itself*, which continues to last, improve, and deepen over time. So fortunate are those who experience deep love, for it is golden beyond measure.

> *Love is our true destiny. We do not find the meaning of life by ourselves alone—we find it with another.*
> —Thomas Merton

Being in Love Combines Both Love and Romance

If you are truly in love, genuine romance is found inside the mind and heart. You care for one another, you give unselfishly, and you share precious moments no matter what is going on around you. If love and caring are missing, all the romance in the world will make little difference.

On the unfortunate side, some people mistake romantic actions or sexual attraction for love and may quickly jump into a commitment only to find that the relationship is shallow and meaningless. Some get married anyway, perhaps thinking, "This is as good as it gets," "Maybe no one else will want me," or "Things will change after we are married," none of which are good reasons for making such a commitment.

While chemistry and physical attraction are usually part of getting together, really being in love involves "knowing," plus absolute commitment to the heart and soul of each other. Of course, people can grow together and increase their love over time, as witnessed by cultures with arranged marriages, or those who get married for other reasons. But dedication and caring for the other person are essential.

Being in love is also much more than just performing romantic actions. When expressed sincerely with no thought of getting anything in return, love can produce a profound sense of bonding and unity. When both romance and love are present, the richness of the relationship has the capacity to increase many times over.

And Then There Is Marriage

A perfect marriage is just two imperfect people who refuse to give up on each other.
—Unknown

Many people today question, "Why marriage? We can just live together and get out of it if we need to." That is a very common scenario, and many couples do just that. In fact, in a sense, the institution of marriage is under siege. Marriage used to be a given, while today it is a choice. That may be a good thing, because to bring a child into a world where parents will later separate is not the best thing for a child.

People give lots of reasons for getting married—security, to make things official, he's really cute, she's really sexy, he has a good job, my family likes him, the clock is ticking and I want a baby, etc. Individually, these are not very sound reasons. Marriage is bigger than both individuals, and it is wise to have many good reasons for marriage. Two of the main ones are compatibility and similar values.

Most couples marry because they love each other. Many have a strong belief in God and have made a commitment before Him. They desire to create a loving, stable, and enduring life together. Regardless of beliefs, marriage somehow elevates their promises to a true union of hearts, minds, and souls which is usually greater than just living together. In essence, without marriage, it's much easier to give up when things become difficult.

The Desire to Work Things Out

The real key to a good marriage is the absolute and unmitigated intention to work things out when differences and problems occur, which they surely will. This means that partners feel safe sharing their feelings, knowing they will be heard, and trusting that they will still be cared about if they disagree. If those objectives are not present, all the love and romance in the world will not keep the marriage flourishing.

Oftentimes, individuals have a need to be "right" or get their own way. They want their partner to concede so that they can have things as they wish. This does not show a readiness to consider the other's needs. And so, letting go of the need to be right, plus a strong commitment to the relationship, are essential. Having a good marriage takes nurturing one another, planning out your lives, and making your relationship a priority. Assessing why you are together and deciding what you want from your marriage by setting goals will help you immensely. If those things are in place, then love and romance can blossom.

Love and Romance

Romantic actions added to love tend to create more love, which creates more romance, which creates more and deeper love, and on and on. The flow moves back and forth in a delicious dance, engendering more profound and rich feelings for both individuals.

She sways with joy as she does the morning dishes. He walks to the car with a jaunty step. She nurses the baby, excited he will be coming home soon. He solves a financial problem at work, knowing she will validate his creativity. When they disagree about the new television he just bought, they confidently express their differences of opinion and resolve things amicably.

Many older couples say their love grows more profound over time in their golden years. They have stuck together, weathered the storms, remained committed to one another, and fostered their love and romance.

Diane was a colleague of mine. When her husband was just 52 years old, he died of a sudden heart attack. They were deeply in love, and she missed him terribly. One day, she volunteered some of the things he did to demonstrate love.

"He did little romantic things like placing a rose on my pillow, tucking a love note in my makeup drawer, or putting a heating pad in the bed to warm my feet. I know a heating pad doesn't sound very romantic, but it was to me. It was so special, and was just about the most romantic thing he could have done for me."

To put it all together, love becomes profound when romance, affection, and deep gratitude exist simultaneously. Everything expands in a rich and magical way.

How Long Will the Honeymoon Last?

Unfortunately, it doesn't. For most, there is no way to sustain that magical feeling, that lust, that yearning. It just isn't logical or realistic. Relationships shift and fluctuate because real life happens. People become so involved in daily pursuits that they become distracted by all there is to do.

Even in the best of partnerships, it is easy to gradually begin taking one another for granted, and the romance and excitement that were once at such a high pitch may die down. Traits which were charming in the beginning come to be annoying, tedious, or downright unacceptable. For example:

- *His hard-working habits that she highly valued turn into, "He's never home, and everything is always up to me."*
- *Her love and devotion for her family, which he found extremely appealing, becomes, "Why does she talk to them all the time and run to fix their every problem?"*
- *His love of sports becomes, "There's never any us time because you watch every conceivable game that was ever invented using a ball."*
- *And her love of cooking and fixing good meals becomes, "You're so obsessed with buying everything organic and spending hour upon hour in the kitchen. No wonder our budget is shot."*

Dates and outings that used to happen all the time when you went out together alone, without friends or family, may occur only once a month or not at all. The flowers he used to bring cease to grace the living room, and his favorite meals come out of the oven only on special holidays.

It's not something to fear. It's just something to be aware of and not panic when you don't have the same gushy feelings you had earlier on. Your love *can* grow, and you *can* keep the romance going, even when pregnancy takes a toll on mom-to-be and when dad-to-be is all stressed out for many reasons yet to be discussed.

Unfortunately, many couples tend to let the romantic actions die away because they stop *being and doing* love. Life then can easily become ordinary and unromantic. But you can keep that momentum going even during stressful and difficult times. It takes awareness, conscious effort, playfulness, and attention to keep moving in a positive direction instead of just existing, being roommates, and absentmindedly going about life. Even if love has diminished but a solid commitment is present, the love that was lost can usually be nurtured to flourish and grow again.

Moving from Us to Family

It is indeed a big step moving from being a couple to having children, though it can be one of the most wonderful parts of existence. However, if one hasn't moved into the *us* stage, as Chad hadn't in the following example, being a parent will be difficult, and marital happiness will suffer.

Chad thought nothing of going out with his buddies after work two or three nights a week. Sometimes he would come home drunk. On Saturday, he liked to play golf with his dad, and at other times he went to baseball practices and football games and spent limitless time on computer games. Sally told him he behaved just like he did before they were married, and that if he didn't value her and their marriage, she didn't want to be married. However, she was pregnant. She felt boxed into a corner, and couldn't imagine raising a baby on her own. While they were in agreement about having a child, she hadn't expected that Chad would avoid taking responsibility and ignore her so much.

Fortunately she convinced him to go to counseling with her. As we discussed their ideas about marriage, he came to realize that he was indeed acting as though he were still single. He loved Sally and didn't want to lose her, so they came up with strategies of how to be a couple instead of two separate people. Sally made some changes as well, and by the time the baby came, their happiness had increased greatly. They were both ready to be loving parents and a united couple.

All couples are destined to encounter ups and downs. Each person will make untold mistakes and blunders that they will regret. That's just real life, because no one is perfect. But add a pregnancy and a new life to the family, and existence can get pretty crazy. As children come along, there are more chances for differing opinions to erupt.

Many parents suffer a temporary dip following the birth of the baby, at least until the child sleeps through the night. If commitment, love, and understanding are not present, it could take months or years to improve—or never. Surviving the struggle is about a couple's ability to approach issues with kindness, compromise, respectful negotiation, and cooperative problem–solving. So it's advantageous to have knowledge about how to keep love and romance thriving.

> *My clients Fran and Milt used their busy lives of working, caring for their children, serving at church, and Milt being a Scout leader as excuses for their lack of romance. The marriage was in real trouble simply because they didn't take time for each other, which led to a decline in their loving feelings and actions. It took a while, but when they made time to go on dates, talk about goals and dreams, and engage in a bit of romance, a spark came back to both their days and their nights. All it took was planning time for what was most important to them—their relationship.*

Some individuals have a difficult time even saying the words "I love you." Others do not appear to be loving or romantic, though they may feel it inside. Perhaps they don't know how to express their feelings or are almost embarrassed by the idea of doing so.

Love Is a Verb

Being in love is a beautiful feeling, but it is also far more. Love is a verb and involves doing and performing actions on behalf of one another. When love is present, you might be doing almost anything and it can seem romantic. Why? It's because you are giving attention and focus to your partner. You are together in the moment, sharing your hearts, feeling gratitude for one another, and looking forward with anticipation to your lives as a couple.

Imagine standing outside with your sweetheart, looking at an enormous, luminous, orange moon coming up over the horizon. You hold one another close, enjoying the beauty, while feeling deep love and thankfulness for your lives together.

On the other hand, imagine standing outside looking at the same enormous, luminous, orange moon with a lackadaisical attitude toward one another. Feelings of love, tenderness, and caring are nowhere to be found. You are just looking at another moon or perhaps wondering what to fix for dinner tomorrow night for company. Ho hum, so what?

Indeed, love is much more than just a feeling. When one partner stops *doing* loving things, the *feelings* of love fade. This can lead the other partner to stop doing loving acts, which can easily become a cycle of unhappiness.

In session one day, Josh said, "I've simply fallen out of love with Andi. We are living like roommates. She's different, really shut down, and I just don't know how to get things back." When I asked him what was missing, he said, "I'd love it if she'd meet me for lunch sometimes, or pay attention to me when I come home. She's always too busy with the kids. And mostly she never wants to have sex. I really miss that."

I asked if he'd talked to her about it and he said it was too late for that because they just quarreled a lot and she thought she was giving her all. I then asked what he was doing to meet her needs. "Oh, I help out a lot. I vacuum, I change the baby, I do the dishes. I do a lot of things for her." Then I asked what she had told him she really would like from him. "Oh, she just wants to talk about stuff. I'm usually tired, and talking just gets us in trouble." I suggested that he ask her to tell him some meaningful things he could do for her; then with that information he could implement one or two of them.

He returned two weeks later and said, "It was a miracle. When I asked what she wanted, she said she just wanted me to listen, so I did. I asked her questions and got interested in what she was saying. She also asked me not to try to fix anything, so I didn't. That's a big change—for me, anyway. And the best thing was that she invited me out to lunch, and we had a really nice time. We even made love on Wednesday."

Josh was willing to listen to Andi with sincere interest, and she responded by wanting to spend time with him. She was also more loving. You can see that his small changes made huge differences in the marital dynamic.

One thing Josh did not understand was that Andi wanted *connection* with him more than she wanted the *help* he provided. When he gave lovingly, knowing her most important needs, he got a better response. That didn't mean he should stop helping with the chores; but as he discovered her deeper desires, his efforts were appreciated, and his own needs were met. There is much more to discuss about this topic in Chapter X, in the section "7 Keys to Your Sweetheart's Heart."

So, think of some things you might do, jot down a few ideas, then put them in your underwear drawer, so that every time you change, you can remember some meaningful ways to show love. Shake things up a bit. Find out what your partner would love for you to do; then do the unexpected. What you perform doesn't have to be huge. It could be as simple as taking her car to the carwash, bringing her a box of chocolates, giving him a nice foot rub, or making his favorite dessert.

Romance added to love is one of the important elements to keeping a marriage alive, energetic, bright, robust, and exciting, as opposed to dead, inactive, dull, boring, and weak. Love increases romance, which increases love, and so it goes in an ever–expanding circle. What kind of relationship do you want? The choice is yours, so set goals for your relationship.

Do you want your love to grow or to stagnate? When most people get married, they think that everything will work out just fine because they are in love. They let things move along on autopilot, without a plan. Actually, I strongly believe that having goals for your relationship is critical. Many give far more time to creating business plans, planning a trip to Europe, making meal menus, or designing their financial future. But if your marriage is unhappy, you will likely be unhappy with the rest of your life.

If you are happy in your marriage, you will have the best chance to be happier in other spheres of your life. And your children will have the greatest chance for being self–loving, caring, and responsible human beings. So make your marriage your highest priority.

Setting your purposes and goals can be a fun project if you have not already done so. Consider why you are together, what you hope to achieve by your partnership, and how you can attain those things. How do you want it to look and feel? What are your goals for the next 5, 10, and 20 years?

A Silver Lining

Highs and lows will come, but even the darkest cloud has a silver lining. While many unforeseen struggles await, the rewards are immeasurable when they are managed and softened with love, compassion, and respect. Those who are aware of the potential changes that may occur during pregnancy and after childbirth, who learn tools and skills to help mitigate issues, who give one another the benefit of the doubt and develop the ability to work through disappointments and mistakes, will be more apt to overcome challenging circumstances that are sure to occur. Never forget that you always have choices.

Sid and Elli were married for five years before they decided to get pregnant. They were both working and had a reasonably happy life; but as Elli's pregnancy progressed, Sid became more irritable. He felt all the attention was on her, and it made him angry when her parents catered to her "every whim." His level of understanding went in the dumpster, and he began to ignore her complaints. Not that they were excessive; he just wanted her to be "normal" again.

They both wanted the baby, but Sid was not expecting all the changes they encountered. When they sought counseling, they were both angry and were considering a separation. But as they learned what was actually "normal" in the new paradigm, they were able to rekindle their feelings and move forward; plus, they learned how to express themselves, understand one another, and accept their differences. The new choices they decided to make vastly improved their relationship.

Information is powerful, and assistance of many kinds can help you through the adventure and carry you on to an even stronger marriage—provided you work and play together, especially through the difficult times. There are many ways to prevent damage in the first place when the going gets rough, and fortunately there are equally many ways to repair hurts that may already have occurred. An abundance of ideas on how to stay in love are discussed throughout this book.

Creating a Solid Foundation

The most important step in creating a solid foundation is having a thriving relationship with a person whom you deeply love, trust, and respect and who treats you with love, honor, and respect. A dear friend of mine recently lost her husband. Though she is grieving severely for her beloved, she mentioned a few of the things listed below that she and her husband did on a regular basis that kept their marriage impassioned. If you want a strong marriage, you can *decide* together to implement these or some of your own ideas and guidelines:

- Never go to bed angry.
- If you are upset with one another, hold hands and face each other with a desire to work out what is bothering you. Speak kindly while expressing your

feelings and listen to each other attentively. (See Chapter IX on Communication.)

- Never use a harsh or accusatory tone.
- When one partner leaves the house, always give an ardent kiss.
- When one partner returns, leave what you are doing and greet them with another ardent kiss.
- Hold hands often when out and about, or at home watching a movie, or just talking.
- Go to bed at the same time.
- Snuggle in bed before going to sleep.
- Perform loving acts of kindness daily.

Can you see how implementing these elements could enrich love and leave couples wanting to be together? It would make arguing challenging and provide a solid base for loving harmony. Yes, there are many wonderful benefits.

Love is a decision; it is a judgment; it is a promise. If love were only a feeling, there would be no basis for the promise to love each other forever. A feeling comes and it may go. How can I judge that it will stay forever, when my act does not involve judgment and decision.
—Erich Fromm, *The Art of Loving*

Options for Action

- Review what brought you together in the beginning and made you decide to join your lives together.
- Talk about what you did previously to nurture your relationship.
- Share what you would like to continue or renew.
- Discuss what love and marriage mean to you now.
- Chat about your progress in moving from Me to Us.
- Write down specific ways you like love and romance shown to you. Then discuss your lists about ways to add more acts of love and romance.
- Discuss your goals, desires, hopes, and dreams for your future. Talk about ways you might attain these things together.
- Look at how committed you are to the relationship and if you are willing to work things out, even when life gets tough.
- Create time to be together no matter how busy life becomes.
- Every day do some acts of kindness for one another.
- Focus on your partner's strengths.

Chapter II
The Joys and Challenges
of Having Children

Parenting is the biggest sacrifice one can make. It's putting your life on hold to fulfill the promise of your children's tomorrow.
—Frederica Ehimen

"That moment when first I held you in my arms was amazing beyond belief. As I looked into your beautiful blue eyes, I wanted to gaze at you endlessly, cherishing the miracle that God had given your daddy and me. The promise we hold for your life is full of joy and hope. You will always be dear to our hearts. I only pray that we as parents may be guided to raise you to feel deeply loved, happy, and self-assured. You are a rich blessing, and I thank God for bringing you into our lives."

These are the feelings I had when my first baby was born. The sentiments for my other three children and later my grandchildren have been equally profound.

We're Having a Baby!

At the stage when you find out you are having a baby, you are full of questions and bursting with feelings. "It's real; we're going to have a baby. Will it be a boy? Will it be a girl? How do we prepare? Will we be good parents? How will we adjust? I'm scared, but I'm so excited. Can we do this? Yes, we can! Oh, I love you so much!"

The emotions are plentiful, all the way from enthusiasm to insecurity, exhilaration to apprehension, delight to fright. You've probably started thinking about how to get baby's room ready, looking up possible names, picking out cribs and clothes, and generally rejoicing. Family members are thrilled for you, and if there are other children in the family, they will be jumping with excitement, too, in anticipation of a little brother or sister coming into the world. Of course jealously may get the best of them later on, but right now, there's no competition as long as the baby is inside. The real fun will begin soon enough.

As the mother–in–waiting, you have been seeing the doctor, perhaps getting ultrasounds, and watching and feeling what is going on inside you. That first ultrasound photo is something you will both treasure and want to send out to everybody. It will likely be the first thing you put in baby's scrapbook so you can always remember that first real sign of life in the womb.

Your expectations are glorious, and you can hardly wait until that little one begins to squirm. At first there will be a gentle flutter, then little nudges, and gradually great thuds. "Come on, let me out. I want to play," baby seems to say. Or the message of one who wants to delay the process might be, "It's crowded in here, but it's warm and safe, and I'll stay until I'm good and ready."

If you are a first–time father, you may be wondering how this new child will change your life and your relationship with your spouse. You're enthusiastic, but you may be anxious and overwhelmed by all the extra responsibilities and pressures, not to mention the additional expenses for clothes, a crib, stroller, car seat, decorating the room, showers, birth announcement, and on and on.

"You mean I have to get up in the night with the baby?" can either be a disheartening concept or a temporarily joyful thought. You're probably also worried about getting enough sleep to go to work in the morning. Are you exhausted yet?

Celebrating the Arrival

Nothing is more rewarding than being a parent.
—Anonymous

Finally—the birth. Such ecstasy, such wonder, such fulfillment when you see she has ten tiny fingers and ten tiny toes or he has a nose just like his daddy. Whew, everything is normal. What a marvelous little bundle of joy. His silky skin and big brown eyes, her rosebud lips and the soft fuzz of hair on top of her beautiful head. When you really think about it, conceiving, incubating, and delivering a real human being is a miracle.

The excitement is remarkable, and nothing in the entire world could be more extraordinary. The naming, blessing, christening, welcoming ritual, and all the festivities create much elation for the whole family. And it's likely that being involved together every step of the way with your husband or wife will create a beautiful bond.

But Then Overwhelm

Aside from all the fun and anticipation, most first–time parents have no idea what is to come, even if they have read books, done babysitting, or have socialized with people who have kids.

First off, one day you will remember that you incorrectly thought the baby would just fit beautifully into your current existence. No problem, right? Wrong! You will find out rather quickly that your life is no longer your own but revolves around the precious child you are both eagerly awaiting. He or she will need your constant attention and round–the–clock care, at least for a while. So it's best to be prepared for a total change!

Wouldn't it be nice if babies came with instructions pinned to the umbilical cord? But since they don't, it doesn't take long for life to suddenly become very demanding. New parents are often astonished at how much that little "cargo" can change their lives—not just for the moment, but forever. The moment the baby is born, life will be different. The transformation will occur in physical, mental, emotional, sexual, social, relational, financial, logistical, and spiritual arenas. Each child compounds the areas of change and scope of responsibility.

Remember when you were single? Ah, the romance! You were probably tender, starry–eyed, and dreamily romantic. And as newlyweds, few things kept you from working all day and playing all night. You had freedom to visit acquaintances, have friends to dinner, go on vacations, and do almost anything you wanted—including impromptu sexy moments, exotic escapades, and amorous trysts on top of a mountain.

Then there was the allure of self–determination and lack of constraints—spending money, buying yet another splashy car, having the latest trendy fashions, and so on. I really do hate to disappoint, but a lot of that will come to a rapid cessation—hopefully to be taken up at a later time. Even though that day will probably return, many people change so much that events that once had great value no longer seem important. Children can do that to parents, but rewards for the trade–offs are countless.

Those Lovely Hormones

A mother's hormones can get rather whacky and may be that way from conception until she stops nursing, maybe longer. Life can be a real roller coaster. She feels tired and is often dreadfully out of sorts, moody, temperamental, and high strung. You never know what will set her off into an emotional twitter. She may even want peanuts, ice cream, or popcorn in the middle of the night. But being a loving partner, I'm sure you will run right out into the dark and stormy night to get what she craves. Yes?

It might be a bit of a surprise to a novice husband—and if not a surprise, a huge disappointment—that most women experience a sharply reduced sex drive during most of their pregnancy. This is due to many factors, but typically it's because of the hormones. You may hear her say, "Sorry, honey, I'm way too tired." If this fact is not kept in mind, the behavioral changes can be misinterpreted as a lack of love. Remember, it's the hormones, just the hormones.

If one partner doesn't feel loved and cherished, problems can develop and escalate. It is unfortunate when couples are quick to let their temporary unhappiness make decisions for them. One of my male clients was on the verge of giving up the marriage because his wife was so unresponsive to his sexual needs. Wisely, they both sought counseling and learned that some of their discontent could be avoided with a bit of education and understanding of typical circumstances. Therefore, it is my advice to wait until her body has normalized and both of you are getting enough sleep. Things will get dramatically better if you love and care for each other. Sexual desire usually returns.

Who Am I?

Sometimes, after the baby comes, with all the inherent changes and challenges, it is easy to lose sight of yourselves. You may wonder, "Who am I? Where did I go? I've made so many accommodations for the baby and my spouse, I don't know myself anymore." At the same time, it can be a wonderful time of discovery and growth if you open up to it. You are a marvelous human being, so it's important to be gentle and kind with yourself. Take care of YOU; rest, relax, and include activities you enjoy. Create some precious "me" time. I know it will be difficult, but as you care for yourself, you will actually have more of yourself to give to others.

Where Did WE Go?

Having a child can bring your closer, but it can also blemish your relationship if you are not prepared for the potential struggles. Eventually you may begin to miss the couple that you used to be. Where did "we" go? Many couples report that it takes at least a year after the birth of their baby to feel there is space to think of each other as partners. You are now a family with a child, and the dynamic will never be quite the same.

At this point, it's easy to fall victim to the weight of baby's needs for attention and the gaping lack of time to address your own. Life can quickly become ordinary, mundane, and unromantic, as well as full of fatigue, stress, and discouragement. Who has time or energy to feel "in love"? When complexities arise, many individuals are far too willing to allow the distance to persist, or they give up entirely.

And if such thoughts lead to ending the relationship, now it's also about potentially breaking up the family. Contemplating divorce often adds the burden of feeling trapped with no viable choices.

False Expectations

Children, especially babies, never seem to fit into all your expectations. Therefore it is wise to be flexible, for things will never work out exactly as you intended.

First, you must understand the potential obstacles; second, you need to have realistic expectations of yourselves; and third, you must make a firm commitment to one another and give the relationship a chance to succeed until after the initial struggles are over. Don't give up because the going is tough. Equip yourselves with information, tools, and options. Strong determination and enduring patience are also useful.

I advise you to lower your standards and self–expectations for a while. The hardships of having a new baby will pass. You can get back to—well, "normal" is not the word, for things will never be the same as before, but perhaps you will be able to view the new way in a positive manner. Your old life is over, so treasure your new life and make it the best you possibly can.

Just know that the three most difficult areas of stress are: a shortage of sleep, a lack of intimacy, and too many responsibilities with insufficient time or energy to handle them.

If One of You Isn't Celebrating

Sometimes, couples get pregnant without wanting to, or one of the individuals is unhappy while the other is elated. This in and of itself can create stress. Usually, once the baby arrives, everyone is more contented, and gradually the feelings change to gladness. Ideally, I think both parents should be in agreement about having or not having a child or children. Surprisingly, many couples don't even discuss such possibilities or preferences before marriage. This is not something I would advocate, because bringing a child into the world is one of the most important decisions in life.

If you are even slightly in a non–celebratory mood, the greatest feeling is often one of fear, such as: fear I will be like my father, fear I won't be a good parent, or fear the baby will take away my freedom. Some couples believe it is necessary to have their lives in good order before having a child. They want to have adequate finances, a nice home, and extra money in the bank. A "mistake" gets in the way of that. But most people adjust and are very happy about the coming of their baby. Somehow, everything works out. Even the extra expenses are all worthwhile.

However, if an adjustment is not made, happiness may be compromised, and the future may not look bright. The crucial thing is to be willing to consider your ideas together as early as you can, both before and during the pregnancy. Listen to one another's viewpoints calmly and with understanding. Nothing is solved or eased by arguing about the "correctness" of your own emotions. Everyone has personal feelings which should be acknowledged and reasonably discussed.

Adoption Is Wonderful, Too

I hasten to add that adoption is a very precious thing, although quite different from being pregnant. While the experiences will not be the same as carrying one's own child, what a gift it is to provide a loving home to a child who might not otherwise have had the opportunity.

Some families know well in advance when the adoptive child will arrive, while others don't know until the last moment. So it is a good idea to be prepared for the eventuality whenever it comes. Even though not everything in this book will be applicable to adoption, I think most of it will be valuable. Some adoptions fall through at the last minute. This is a sad and difficult blow to prospective parents. Adoptive parents genuinely want their children, or they would not have begun what is usually a laborious and expensive process; however, it is well worth the work and sacrifice. It is critical that the children be told how sincerely they were wanted.

My son Michael and his wife had two wonderful biological children, but they wanted to have more children.

Michael had spent two years in Haiti and witnessed the poverty and corruption of that country. When he and his wife discovered they couldn't conceive again, they chose to adopt a child from Haiti. It was a lengthy process, but James and Sylvie—loving brother and sister—were the absolute favorites in the orphanage, and my son and his lovely wife decided to adopt both of them. When everything was finalized, the children were four and six years old. They are delightful, and we love them dearly. I often reflect on how terrible their lives might have been had they remained in Haiti. And what a blessing it has been, not only to them but to us, to have them in our family.

This is a lovely sentiment from an adoptive parent:

The Day We Adopted You

If we had it to do over again
Adoption is what we'd choose.
We got more than we had hoped for
The day we adopted you.
For you have given us more in life
Than we could ever want or need.
You made our house into a home
And made our family complete.
We love you more than life itself
For all the things you say and do,
And if we had it to do over again
You'd be the only one we'd choose.

Author Unknown

Before you were conceived, I wanted you. Before you were born, I loved you. Before you were here an hour, I would die for you. This is the miracle of life.
—Maureen Hawkins

Options for Action

- Talk about the attitudes you had about having children when you first met and how you feel about that today.
- Discuss your excitement, hopes, fears, and apprehensions about having a baby.
- Shop together for the baby.
- Share your ideas for staying in love and keeping romance alive.
- Talk about ways to support each other after the baby arrives.
- Try to be understanding about the changes in hormones and changes that can occur.
- Share the person(s) you would most like to have help you during the difficult times and how to ask for assistance.
- Discuss ways to keep overwhelm from affecting your relationship. When tiredness or overwhelm set in, ask how you can help relieve the stress. Then do your best to accommodate.
- Find ways to be physically intimate, even if it's not always making love.
- Buy something meaningful for each other to mark this important event.
- Make time for one another to be intimate, talk, and share affection.

Chapter III
Diapers, Dismay, and Disarray

If you let yourself be absorbed completely, if you surrender to the moments as they pass, you live more richly those moments.
—Anne Morrow Lindbergh

Anne Morrow Lindbergh was suggesting that people live in the moment, surrendering to whatever is happening. To surrender means to stop fighting, hiding, and resisting. When you are not living in the present, you miss out on the freedom and peace of the now. Sometimes things just are what they are and need to be accepted.

However, things can change in the future, whether through the passage of time, effort, or finding useful options. So strive for living as richly as possible in the moment. Admittedly, it is challenging to do, especially when life seems absolutely overwhelming.

I Need the Pacifier

"I love Hanna to pieces, but she's up all night wanting to nurse. She cries and cries, and I don't know what to do. I haven't had sleep for days, and my body is worn to a frazzle. And during the day—I can't get anything done. Nothing but soiled diapers, spit-up everywhere, piled up washing, and frustration. Help! Give ME the pacifier."

This was Gretchen's cry, along with thousands of other moms just like her. If it sounds as though she is wishing her little one had never been born, it's not true. Even with all the diapers, dismay, and disarray—as well as disappointment, despondency, dirty dishes, more diapers, daddy troubles, and dishevelment—she wouldn't trade little Hanna or any other baby for all the diamonds in the world. It's just hard, downright tiring, nerve-wracking, and absolutely overwhelming for both parents, not to mention feeling overworked, underappreciated, and definitely underpaid.

Suddenly, life is all about logistics—feeding, changing diapers, doing laundry, handling household responsibilities, earning a living, and on and on. Conflicts become more prevalent, and there is less time for sexual intimacy and meaningful conversation. Parents have to juggle which one can sleep for a few hours when the baby is comfortable and adequately fed—yet howling, for some unknown reason.

But just so you know, rarely do people wish their baby had never come. It's a life–altering experience, one with joy, gladness, and true life–purpose. The journey of self–discovery and development of a new way of life with one's partner is unmatched.

Make a Plan

Lots more ideas will follow, but to get you started, I hope you will create a plan of all the things you have to do. Discuss your individual and joint expectations, and then assign tasks. The reason many couples don't make a plan before their first baby arrives is because they don't anticipate how demanding it can really be.

Arguments over who should do what and when can cause immense misery, as in the following example of Saundra and Vick:

Saundra couldn't understand why Vick couldn't anticipate her needs. "You expect me to do everything. Can't you see that the dishes need to be done when I'm nursing the baby?" Vick's response was, "Just tell me what needs to be done." Saundra retorted, "Can't you just see? I shouldn't have to ask you to do everything. Just do something around here."

You might imagine that Saundra's cutting remarks were not well received. Vick, like many men, was willing to help but needed to be told what to do. But when she yelled at him, he was less inclined to want to assist her. She was advised to be kind, as well as more forthcoming with her requests. When she did, he was more than willing to comply. He also earned voluminous "points" by learning to anticipate what needed to be done.

Many men aren't good at anticipating their wife's needs. Their thoughts are on work, bills, or other matters on their own to-do lists. Stress and squabbling add to a couple's unhappiness and will accumulate and escalate over time; so learn to work it out so that both parties are content. If that means making more requests, do that. If it means upping your ability to see what needs to be done, do that.

Obviously, there are countless inherent and unanticipated tough situations that can place stress and strain on a relationship. Just normal everyday living for the first few weeks can be a struggle. And getting adequate rest and sleep at this stage can be tricky. Especially arduous is the intense stress that can occur in couples who have a premature, ill, or special needs child. More about this is to come.

It's the unusual baby who smiles and coos all the time and gently wakes in the night once or twice and peacefully falls back to sleep. Lucky you if your baby is like this. No matter what, you will look back and treasure those moments: good or bad, invigorating or exhausting.

Ask for Help

Before going to the hospital, it's a good idea to line up help for when you come home, if at all possible. Though hubby may be there, he may not be able to take much time away from work. Family members can be a great relief, as can friends and neighbors, if they are willing. Most mothers of their pregnant daughters want to be present, but if they don't come to your rescue, ask other family members or friends, or hire someone if you can afford to do so. It's especially energy–consuming if there are other children at home, though they can be a big help. Even a two–year–old can fetch a diaper. But certainly that won't be nearly enough help.

My family was awesome. I think I would have fallen in a heap without my mother, sister, aunt, mother–in–love, or sister–in–love coming when I had a new baby or just to help out. (I proudly call my in–laws my "in–loves" because in–law sounds so cold. My mother–in–law, whom I adored, started this tradition by calling me her "daughter–in–love." I have continued this with my family, and they have adopted it, too.) They were truly life–savers, especially for my husband after our second child was born. I was hospitalized for six week with a serious blood clotting condition and numerous complications. It was a tough time for him, and without assistance, I don't think he could have managed the family, household, and his work.

Simplify Your Life

It took until I had my third child to decide that I didn't have to be "Molly Homemaker." Though it was difficult, I let many things go that I thought I absolutely had to do in order to be a good wife and mother. I also learned, through much self–talk and support from friends, not to be hard on myself. Believe me, that was a struggle for a while. Later on, I was able to return to keeping things up as I had before. It made life much easier for my family, and I was definitely a happier person when I let go.

Can You Spoil Your Baby?

This is a question people ask over and over. Many parents are afraid that their children will grow up to be dependent, spoiled, or needy. Historically, crying babies were allowed to continue to cry endlessly, and there was actually a "hands–off" mentality. Some would say, "If you pick up Junior, you will spoil him forever." Today, the theory is much different. Many studies have shown that children who are deprived of touch or who are left to cry endlessly experience developmental delays and other problems. Babies need all the care and attention you can give to them as demonstrated by physical contact, loving attention, and emotional reassurance.

Since babies cry to communicate their needs for food, comfort, diaper changes, or just wanting to be held, responding to those needs promotes in them a sense of security and self-worth. Use your best instincts, and don't let others influence you by saying you are going to spoil your baby. Of course, as a child grows older, he can be indulged to such a degree that he does indeed become dependent, spoiled, or needy. So later on, be aware of balancing appropriate dependency and independence. But as for babies, I don't agree that they will be spoiled if they are loved.

Bonding

Bonding with a parent or caregiver is the first experience a baby will have leading to healthy relationships. Through singing and talking by both parents, bonds can form even before the baby is born. Even though you are not thinking about it now, early bonding will help your children become more secure and well-developed as adults, because it creates safety, security, and increased self-esteem.

After birth, hold your babies, sing to them, talk to them, and let them feel your inner heart. Touching is critical. As they get older, you can read books, pretend, play games, and let them "help" you do daily household activities. They love this. Later on? Uh, not so much.

School-age kids engage in sports, dancing on daddy's feet, piggy back rides, and doing things you love together, as well as being "allowed" to do chores. Keep it fun. Turn off the TV and other devices and focus on connecting. Family rituals, such as having dinner together, family nights, movie/game times, and reading stories before bed are great bonding activities. Most important, say you love them every day—many times, in fact—and strengthen your 1:1 time with each of them.

Feeding

Bottle–feeding is a fine option if necessary. There is nothing like snuggling your baby while he or she is eating, regardless of whether you are breast– or bottle–feeding. Just take those precious moments to be with your baby rather than propping a bottle up in the crib.

I still had a year to go before graduating from the university when my husband and I got married. The diaphragm my mother made certain I had before the wedding day didn't do its duty, and I got pregnant two months after we said our vows. My parents weren't at all happy, but we were delighted—after the initial shock, that is. I was determined to finish my degree, even though my final semester began when my firstborn was only three weeks old. My husband was a Naval officer. I couldn't postpone my schooling because we were going to be sent to Japan immediately after graduation.

School was too far away for me to breastfeed, and so I was unable to have that pleasure. We found a retired nurse who cared for Theresa while I attended classes. We called her Mrs. Snip–a–nipple, because she would snip all the bottle nipples (rather, she made gashes), causing my poor baby to glug down her formula. I'd buy new ones and she would snip them again, even though I asked her not to. Theresa wasn't in any danger, but it was most annoying, so I hid the ones *I* wanted to use in a drawer. After I obtained my degree, I was happy to be able to feed my baby as I desired, though I was very grateful for the babysitter's help.

Unfortunately, I couldn't nurse my second child, either, because of a serious illness. However, I had the beautiful experience of doing so with my last two babies. I cherished the times I could read to them and snuggle them while they were nursing. We loved reading Dr. Seuss and other stories and all being together. What special moments!

My advice is to opt for breast–feeding if at all possible. Even if you can only do so for the first few days, you will provide your baby with that first "vaccine" of valuable colostrum. It is highly concentrated, easy to digest, and provides protection from harmful bacteria and other illnesses. After the first few days, the colostrum changes into thinner, more plentiful milk with important nutrients that provide further protection.

On the other hand, getting your baby to nurse can be stressful for some first–time moms and can create some very tense moments. Sometimes, the hospital staff may not be terribly helpful, as with Natalie:

Natalie was in the hospital for a mere ten hours after her first baby was born. Insurance! Neither mom nor babe knew how to get the milk flowing, and her "army sergeant" nurse wasn't helping. "Nothin's wrong! You got all the right equipment, girl," she said as she shoved tiny Jason onto his mommy's breast.

At home, getting that boy to suck wasn't happening. Poor Natalie sobbed and sobbed and felt absolutely helpless. A nurse acquaintance helped them get the hang of it, and contentment finally reigned. Nursing went much more easily after the births of her other babies; however, her job was not easy with other little ones to care for as well, five in all. Thank goodness for a wonderful husband who was an awesome help, as well as her mother.

Some couples decide for mom to pump her milk once in a while so hubby can bottle feed the baby during the night.

Where's the Romance?

Your baby may be a contented little lamb, or she may be a hungry, demanding, wailing puppy who constantly needs something—exactly what, you don't know. For the first several weeks, and sometimes for months, there is no free time and no opportunity to recharge your drained batteries. The fatigue is gargantuan for both of you, and your days are buried under stacks of laundry, dishes, wet and poopy diapers, a messy house, doctor appointments, going to work, balancing the budget, and other routines of life.

And romance? It is no wonder Mom's sex drive is gone. Maybe it's not until after baby begins to sleep through the night and her body feels rested and healed that she begins to think about the needs of her husband. And that's a sad thing. Some doctors recommend not having intercourse for several weeks before and after the arrival of the baby. While this can seem like an eternity, the time is short in the scheme of things. Your doctor may have a different idea, so be sure to check.

Fortunately, the lack of sexual intimacy is usually temporary; so, husbands, hang in there. Small moments of affection and caring will keep the love fires burning, so don't neglect giving stolen hugs, backrubs, snuggling, or just commenting on how beautiful she looks. And any help with chores will give you mega points. Some new moms experience desperation, sadness, and even post–partum depression (discussed later). Her willingness to communicate may also suffer, largely because of overwhelm and fatigue. Your understanding and support will be greatly valued.

This was Anna's plight:

"I honestly don't know how I can give one more thing. I love Alan with all my heart, but I'm doing the best I can. Sometimes it feels like it's all about him, his needs, his ego. I just have too much responsibility with the rest of the family and the baby, keeping up the house, nursing. I don't know what to do, because I feel I am losing touch with him, but I'm so darn tired I don't have much left for him. Besides that, how can I be both a mom and a lover when I have to give my all to the baby, at least right now?"

Here is the essence of my reply:

I really do get that you are having a tough time. There aren't enough hours to get everything done, and the demands on you are tremendous. At the same time, the man you fell in love with has needs, too. You don't want him to start spending more time at the office or thinking the secretary down the hall is really cute, do you? I'm not saying that would happen, but you just may want to think about ways you can keep him wanting to come home to you. It is quite possible to be both a mom and a lover. People have been doing it for centuries. You need to talk about things together, share your feelings, and see what you can do to work things out so you both get your needs met. If he feels like staying away, he won't be there to help you or give you the companionship you need, so make it viable for the two of you. Never minimize his feelings. They are as real as yours. I'll help you come up with some strategies.

Fathers in the Shadows

Not only can a father get left in the shadows because of all the attention his wife and baby receive, but he can feel like a gorilla on a tightrope. When he gets up with the baby in the middle of the night but still has to go to work, his body may feel as though he fell off the tightrope onto the hard ground. I'm not saying he shouldn't be involved, because he should, but it's important to take his own struggles into account, too.

One mother I know regularly woke her husband up just to burp the baby. She thought that was "only fair." Believe me, Dad will have plenty of chances to help when the baby won't go back to sleep or keeps everyone up with colic or an earache. Somebody's got to get some sleep, and if he has to go to work, please don't wake him up just to give the baby a burp. However, do ask for help as needed, and be sure to thank him. Men love to be appreciated.

Don't be surprised if he experiences his own depressed mood. Some fathers are impatient with all the crying and may not have the "tolerance gene" many moms have. Others have a problem relating well to infants until they are old enough to communicate.

Jerold told me, "I wasn't sure I even wanted a baby, but Margo did, and so I relented. Now I wouldn't trade the little bugger for anything. It's really hard to stay grumpy when he laughs and coos at me. Like the other day, he seemed to enjoy the fact that he sprayed my face with you know what when I changed his poopy drawers. Yup, he's pure delight—well, most of the time—and sometimes I even miss him when he finally goes to sleep."

Yes, the joys are often present and available; but when you're both stressed out and worn thin, arguments and unhappiness can and will erupt. You may start wondering where love and desire went. It didn't go anywhere. It's just hiding somewhere under the bed, not on it.

Do Not Neglect Him

Being in love requires action. So, Mom, I can't stress this enough. Even though you don't feel like it, do not neglect your husband. He wants to feel important, emotionally connected, and dearly loved as much as you do. And he has a strong need to be romantically and sexually intimate. Even when you're tired, there are innumerable ways to make him happy, so be creative.

And don't forget to provide generous love and thanks whenever he helps you. Yes, you have expectations and want him to do things just because they need to be done. Most men are very willing to help, but they usually want to be asked, and they thrive on praise and feeling valued, even for small gestures. I'm sure you want that as well, but you will be happy you gave him what he needs when he returns the kindness to you. It's all worth it, isn't it? There is nothing more wonderful than family.

> *A home with a loving and loyal husband and wife is the supreme setting in which children can be reared in love and righteousness and in which the spiritual and physical needs of children can be met.*
> —David A. Bednar

Self-Care and Self-Love

Before moving on any further, I want to talk about self-care and self-love, which should not be disregarded, whether you're male or female. Sadly, a huge number of individuals in our society have experienced some type of neglect, lack of support, disrespect, disparagement, humiliation, abuse, or severe trauma. This has usually taken place in childhood from a parent, sibling, teacher, friend, or relative. Even one such adverse event can color a person's life; but when it is ongoing, it becomes even more serious and can create lasting feelings of pain, lack of self-assurance, low self-confidence, or even self-hatred.

The reasons for such negative effects are that children tend to take seriously the words and actions of those who are significant to them and may even invent conclusions which are grossly false and self-demeaning. In their innocence, they are unable to make mature, reasonable decisions or understand what is happening to them. They conclude that what is said and done must be accurate and is their fault. Afterwards, they may create a negative view of themselves that lasts until it is understood from an adult perspective later on.

Though many people don't choose to delve into what might have caused or is presently creating destructive patterns or negative attitudes, I want to encourage you toward a healthy exploration in order to lay a foundation for a happy life and a well–functioning family. As you learn to take care of and love yourself, you will have more to give to others. In addition, you won't interpret a look or a word that is not meant to offend as hurtful, offensive, or degrading. You will have self–confidence, so as not to become easily insulted, even in the face of someone who is intentionally trying to hurt you.

When you understand and love yourself, you will have greater love and compassion for those around you. And most important, you will want to do the best job you can, so your children will become strong, self–loving, and responsible adults. If you did not have healthy, supportive people in your life growing up, you can certainly change the patterns and create a life that you did not have. And if you had a healthy, happy childhood, you were very fortunate. You can model your life after those who were significant examples to you. If you have ongoing challenges with your self–concept, counseling can be very effective.

How Children Benefit from a Happy Marriage

The greatest favour we can do our children is to give visible examples of love and esteem to our spouse. As they grow up, they may then look forward to maturity so they too can find such love.
—Eucharista Ward, author of several books, including *A Match for Mary Bennet*

A happy marriage is not only good for you, your health, and your serenity; it is also beneficial for your children.

Children tend to thrive in an environment where there is peace at home, they feel loved and cherished, and they can see that their parents love and respect one another.

Kim was a young stay–at–home mother with three young children. Whenever Ralph came home from work, she would call to the children to come and kiss Daddy, even if they were in the middle of drawing, reading a book, or playing with a friend. She would stop cooking dinner or even nursing the baby so that her husband would feel welcomed and know he was loved and missed. On Saturdays, when she went out with a friend or shopping for groceries, he did the same for her. The children developed this habit, and it helped them to know that their parents were close, which made them feel safe and secure. Best of all, it gave them a good model for their own special relationships later in life.

Certainly, children hope, even assume, that the promises you made at the altar will be lasting. They take for granted that they will grow up in a happy, intact family—that is, until they see classmates' parents getting a divorce. This may cause them to feel insecure and create fear that such a thing could happen to their family.

Witnessing unhappiness between their parents at any time can cause them to feel despondent and anxious. Ongoing, unresolved conflict between parents is detrimental and contributes to children acting out, withdrawing, being rebellious, experiencing low self–esteem, regressing, and being affected by developmental delays. It is therefore imperative to find ways to reduce conflict. Divorce is in most cases a dismal occurrence for children. Though most children do not have memories of their life before the age of three, they receive impressions which can last a lifetime. Even in utero, a baby can sense anger, depression, quarrelling, or unhappiness. Obviously they pick up on these things from birth onward.

> *Never lose sight of who came first—your spouse or your children. If you don't deal with the challenges you could lose the love you once had.*
> —Honoré de Balzac

E. Mark Cummings, a professor of psychology at the University of Notre Dame, said: "Conflict affects children by affecting their sense of emotional security about the family…. A child has a sense of security or well–being, and if they don't have that they feel distressed emotionally, and are more prone to aggression and hostility."

And yet, not all conflict is damaging to children. If they observe their parents being emotionally controlled and see that they are able to *successfully resolve* some distressing situations, their emotional distress is minimized, and they will have more trust that their family is stable and secure. However, if arguments are intense or the situation is inappropriate for children's ears, it is advisable to discuss such matters in private. Kept secrets, stuffed feelings, unshared dreams, or unresolved problems can create worse problems later. Couples need to communicate and do it fittingly so they do not create lasting or irreparable damage to their relationship or to their children.

Those couples who arm themselves with information, get counseling, attend workshops, or talk with professionals and close associates have the best chance of being happy. Couples who pray together as well as play together may have the best chance to stay together. A happy marriage will promote positive development in children and aid their emotional well–being, physical growth, and psychological progress.

> *We cannot teach people anything. We can only help them discover it within themselves.*
> —Galileo Galilei

Options for Action

- Using some of the ideas suggested above, assess together how well you are meeting one another's needs. If you are afraid to be open and honest, look at Chapter IX on how to communicate effectively. It may take some practice.
- Talk about what kinds of help are needed from others and each other and make plans to provide it.
- Talk together concerning feelings about breastfeeding or not.
- Write down ways you can take care of yourselves, do things you enjoy, and get appropriate sleep, rest, exercise, and nutrition.
- Come up with ways and times you can show more affection.
- Talk about methods to mitigate stress.
- Turn down her bed and fluff up her pillow when she's taking care of the baby.
- Write a love message to him and put it under his pillow or on the mirror.
- Watch a romantic movie together, sitting close or snuggling.
- If your honey is on a business trip, arrange for a fruit basket, wine bottle, or something nice to be delivered to the room with a love note.
- Put a mint or cookie on your sweetheart's pillow.
- Give unexpected compliments.

Chapter IV
The Importance of Being DAD

When I was a boy of fourteen, my father was so ignorant I could hardly stand to have the old man around. But when I got to be twenty-one, I was astonished at how much he had learned in seven years.
—Mark Twain

Yes, you dads do get smarter as you age. Don't we all! I'm sure even Mark Twain did. As he said, it is astonishing how much wisdom you gain as you grow older.

Dads, I want to stress that this chapter is especially for you. I hope you already know that YOU are valuable beyond measure, both as a husband and as a father.

As far as parenting is concerned, women seem to groove in right away. It's their natural instinct. However, becoming a father is a role that many men take time to grow into. You may be amazed at how much you will learn and how much both your spouse and children will appreciate you over time as you put in the time and effort. So never underestimate your importance.

Husbands and Dads Matter

As a husband, you are the paramount source of love and strength for your wife. You are her comforter, provider, confidant, problem–solver, lover, and friend. The praise and appreciation you give to her will keep your relationship rich and strong.

As a father, you are a role model, nurturer, coach, problem–solver, playmate, and so much more. Being majorly involved in your children's lives has a huge impact on their social, psychological, and educational development. As you will discover, it takes great commitment as well as time. However, being a parent is certainly among the greatest turning points in a man's life, and it is one that can be filled with abundant joy and satisfaction.

In our society today, many men are given a back seat when it comes to parenting—not because they aren't good fathers, but because they have been pushed aside, perhaps inadvertently. As I have mentioned, men are often not included in the planning, preparation, and care of a child. Especially when a baby is born, most of the attention is given to mother and baby. In addition, wives frequently exclude their husbands, which is a huge mistake, even if it is often done unconsciously. I think some men stand in the background when they could be more in the foreground, even if that means inserting themselves into the situation in a loving way. That means you can be openly expressive of your desires and needs.

The Meaning of Dad's Presence

You absolutely are an integral part of your child's life. Stop for just a moment and ask yourself, "What is most important about having an active dad in the picture?" You can probably come up with many good reasons why fathers should be profoundly involved with their kids.

Think about whether or not your own father was participating in your upbringing. Was he playing with you, teaching you, taking you to fun and interesting places? What impact did that have upon your life? Was it for better or for worse? Many adults, as well as children, were blessed with fathers who brought meaningful experiences, nurturing, support, and fun into their lives. Those men were present, caring, and participating. Sadly, others had absentee, abusive, or uninvolved fathers.

In 2006, Jeffrey Rosenberg and W. Bradford Wilcox published a U.S. Department of Health and Human Services report, *Fathers and Their Impact on Children's Well-Being.* They stated: "Even from birth, children who have an involved father are more likely to be emotionally secure, be confident to explore their surroundings, and, as they grow older, have better social connections.... From these interactions, children learn how to regulate their feelings and behavior. Children with involved, caring fathers (also) have better educational outcomes."

Indeed, children of engaged fathers are more likely to enjoy school, be more involved in extra-curricular affairs, and get better grades. They also display "a greater ability to take initiative and evidence self-control." The report also said that boys who had a good role model with an involved father were more likely to be good fathers themselves. The opposite was true if someone had a non-present or uninvolved father. However, it is wonderful that many men (and women, too) make a determined effort to use a negative role model to vastly improve upon the life they had as a child by being kind and conscientious parents. And what an exquisite gift that is to their children.

Stay–at–Home Dads

A stay–at–home dad (SAHD) is a father who is the main caregiver of the children. The number has grown to about 1.4 million in the past few years, according to an estimate by Beth Latshaw, PhD, at Appalachian State University. Other estimates are even higher. Sometimes this happens because of a job loss, getting bored with a current job or career, a spouse who makes or has the potential of making more money, or a mutual preference. Many SAHDs have home businesses or work part time at home. If you are a SAHD, the National At–Home Dad Network (http://athomedad.org/) may be a good resource.

Some working men actually express jealousy toward the SAHD. Other men say they wouldn't be capable of doing such a thing, while a few belittle those amazing fathers. Rather insensitive, don't you think? The extent of comments can run the gamut. Many men say, "It takes a great deal of courage to be a stay–at–home father." But most say they wouldn't want to change their situation for anything.

When asked, "What is the best thing about being a SAHD?" most reported that they can watch their children grow, have fun together, and help them learn—something many men don't have a great deal of time to do. The worst statement was, "It's darn hard work, and the kids can drive me crazy." So what's new? With much due respect, guys, that statement sounds just like what stay–at–home moms often say. Some days are just like that.

Single Moms

A fair number of women today believe they can adequately raise a child without a father. The fathers of children born to teen girls often abandon both mom and baby because they don't want to be tied to the financial and day–to–day responsibilities. I was a counselor in a high school teen–parenting program, and unfortunately, only a few of the children's fathers had any involvement whatsoever. Several of the girls even had two or more children from different and uninvolved fathers.

According to the U.S. census of 2010, 9.9 million parents were custodial single moms, and 1.8 million were custodial single dads. Certainly the rising divorce rate has contributed to the increase of single–parent households. However, the latest statistics show that more and more *unmarried* women are choosing to have children. In 1980, 18.4% of all births in the U.S. were to unmarried women. However, in 2008, that rate was 40.6%. In 2009, it was 41.0%. (It has dropped slightly since then. By 2015, it had declined to 40.2%.)

Some women find a "sperm–donor dad" or have success adopting a child on their own. As a result, many single mothers lack the influence of a strong male role model in their child's life. In addition, single women have a tough task raising a child or children alone because they must also work. Moreover, most single women have fewer available resources.

If same–sex moms have a child, it is highly important to seek a strong male influence. The reverse is equally true. Children need the inspiration and encouragement of both sexes in their lives.

So you see, your influence as a father is probably more significant than you might think. Just a gentle reminder: Being a loving husband is the best predictor of being a great dad; so do your very best to stay close to your spouse and to be helpful, respectful, intimate, and caring.

A Few Normal Concerns

I hope you are excited about your fatherhood. Though you are most likely just as capable of learning to be a parent as your spouse, it is normal to have conflicting thoughts and emotions. Some of these may include joy and trepidation, happiness and fear, exhilaration and anxiety, delight and nervousness.

Your first child is usually of most concern because you don't know what to expect. It can feel like an emotional roller coaster, one that can change elevation quickly and without notice. Just know you are not the Lone Ranger. What follows are some of the issues many men experience. If you are a first–time dad, you may have thought about these things and others. Or maybe you haven't been concerned at all. In any case, read on and see if anything registers in your world. And if you have already had your baby, just recall what some of your concerns might have been.

- Will my wife be all right throughout the pregnancy and delivery?
- Will the baby develop normally?
- Will sexual intercourse affect the baby?
- Will my wife even want me, or will our sex life decline forever?
- I've heard that some men are jealous of the baby. What if I'm jealous?

- How involved will she want me to be, and what am I capable of?
- What if she's an emotional mess?
- I'm a little nervous about being in the delivery room, but she says she wants me there.
- Having a baby will cost a bundle of money and won't ever stop. Can we afford it all?
- How will having a baby change our relationship?
- Will I be a good dad?
- How can I juggle everything I'm expected to do?

Okay. Let's take a look at some of these concerns. No one answer fits all, but here are some general ideas that I hope will reduce any stress you may be having.

Normal Pregnancy and Delivery

The majority of pregnancies, births, and in utero development of a baby are quite normal. Of course there are exceptions, and some of those concerns are addressed elsewhere in this book and in many other available references.

WebMD reports: "In 2006, infant mortality was 1.9 deaths for every 1,000 live births when babies were born at 40 weeks. This rate increased to 3.9 per 1,000 live births when a baby was born at 37 weeks...." The article included a caution to refrain from pressuring the doctor to deliver early. Because moms can get very physically uncomfortable during the last four weeks, most women would like to have the baby as soon as possible; but that isn't usually advisable.

Support Her Good Health and Well–Being

The best thing you can do is to remind her to take her pre–natal vitamins, eat a healthy diet, and get plenty of rest and sleep. Exercise is excellent too, although at 32 weeks, climbing a "fourteener," one of our 14,000–foot–high mountains in Colorado, would not be a good idea. Not only would she probably not feel up to it; it wouldn't even be safe. However, walking, most routine tasks, and gentle exercise are still encouraged throughout pregnancy. Oh, and make sure she has plenty of help, especially in the early days after delivery. This could be provided by you, a parent, friend, or hired help. Of course, she will treasure your help most of all, unless you have to be at work.

I remember mopping the kitchen floor and fixing stuffed bell peppers and apple pie a few hours before my water broke with my first baby. It was Friday afternoon, and my husband was just returning from sea duty. Though I had already gone to the hospital when he arrived home, he made it just in time for the birth. I don't recall if he ever enjoyed the great meal I had prepared, or whether he even noticed the clean kitchen floor. Those matters were a long way off our radar. The birth of our beautiful baby, Theresa, was the most important event we could conceive of.

Your Baby's Development

There is no guarantee that your baby will develop normally. Any abnormality is unwanted, but it may be comforting to know that only about 3% of babies have birth defects. Living a healthy life and reducing stress during pregnancy will help a lot. Of course, we know that smoking, drinking alcohol, and consuming street or other inappropriate drugs are absolute no-nos. So if she's not sure she's pregnant, she should absolutely abstain from such substances. Other medications, such as anti-depressant and anti-anxiety prescriptions, must be monitored by a doctor. It won't do any good to worry, so just help her take good care of herself.

Will Making Love Affect the Baby?

Most doctors agree that intercourse in a smooth and normal pregnancy won't harm the baby. The uterine muscles are strong enough to provide protection, and a thick mucus plug seals the cervix, as well. However, keep in mind that some doctors recommend not having sex for a few weeks both before and after delivery, so just discuss this with the doctor.

Will She Want Me, or Will Our Sex Life Decline?

I have included quite a bit about this elsewhere. Her hormones may play a very large part in her sexual desires. However, I've given women advice to consider their husbands' needs and wants as well as their own, so I hope the two of you will work things out between you. Just be sure to be kind and thoughtful when asking for your needs and wants to be met, and respect hers as well. For more information, be sure to read the other sections about this.

> *Love does not consist in gazing at each other but looking in the same direction together.*
> —Antoine de Saint-Exupéry

What If I'm Jealous?

Being jealous can be a rather normal reaction. Just don't be childish about it. As we've said, in the beginning, so much attention has to be given to the baby that it is not uncommon to experience some feelings of envy for the time she devotes to the child. You will feel left out at times, but it's up to you to include yourself as much as possible. If it doesn't work as well as you would want, talk about it. If that doesn't work, get counseling. This is a very vulnerable time for both of you. Keeping the lines of communication clear and open is imperative.

Do not underestimate your possible envy of the baby nuzzling and sucking a certain part of your wife's body. While you probably would never verbalize, "That's mine," you certainly might be thinking it. It may be a while before she wants you to be in that place again. On the other hand, you may be lucky. It all depends.

Will She Include Me?

It is important for her to include you as much as possible in all aspects of the pregnancy. If she doesn't, I can understand how you might become irritable. When feasible, attend various events such as showers (that is, if guys are allowed), doctor's appointments, ultrasounds, and pre–natal and childbirth classes. Also ask to be involved in all the other arrangements, from selecting the nursery room colors to buying clothing and picking out a stroller. Doing things together will increase your intimacy and remove some of the fear. If you feel at all neglected, you must *take responsibility* to be proactive and express your feelings. Convey your wishes about other things, as well. You are half of this most important equation of marriage and parenting!

Generally, just be sensitive to her needs, such as picking things up off the floor for her, lifting heavy items, opening the car door, tying her shoes, or cutting her toenails as her tummy gets bigger. Hugs, back rubs, and hand and foot massages are also delicious for you both; so as you give to her, she will hopefully give back to you.

Will She Be an Emotional Mess?

The short answer is "yes." Talk about roller coaster rides! Her emotions are all over the place, and she is sure to experience some of the same emotions you are feeling—and more! This can be challenging. Do your best to assuage her concerns, anxieties, and fears. Ask how you can help her. I promise that this will go a long way toward her feeling your love and support. Fortunately, her emotional mess will be temporary—that is, until her hormones level out. So hang in there.

Use your creativity to imagine all the ways you can increase romance. You can call her on the phone or text love messages during the day, send flowers, buy surprise baby gifts, plan an exciting adventure, get something special for her to wear (even sexy undies or nightwear), go on dates that *you* plan, tell her she is beautiful, and always make her feel special. You can keep romance alive even if she feels shut down for a while. Don't allow that to affect your whole life together.

My client Tim had some significant concerns:

"Though I know Tess is tired, I'm tired, too. She just doesn't get it. I sometimes get up with the baby and take care of the other kids, and then I have to go to work all day. I'm depressed, overworked, and overwhelmed with all the extra responsibilities I have, too. And the money is going out the door like filings to a magnet. It's all really getting me down. One minute she's happy, the next she's crying or gets really cross at me. At work, I don't have problems like a crying baby, a frustrated wife, and a messy house. Sometimes I don't even want to come home."

For sure, a distracted, despondent, tired, overwhelmed, hormonal wife is a lot to handle. And the baby's screaming and "letting loose"—both top and bottom—can create mental and physical distress. My advice to Tim was to be open and communicate with her. A kind and gentle approach would help her avoid defensiveness, although certainly no one could guarantee her reaction. Those hormones were probably kicking up.

And while it was important for him to engage in what he wanted, I cautioned him to strive for patience. I said that once the baby slept through the night, the situation would improve. He wouldn't be so frustrated and overworked. In addition, if he was loving, helpful, understanding, and kind, her sexual feelings and concerns for him would probably return.

Had I been able to talk to Tess—who didn't come in—I would have told her that even though she was exhausted, the man she fell in love with had needs, too. She should continue to be a loving wife as well as a mother, even when it seemed there was nothing left to give. There are many ways to be loving and romantic, so I would have suggested that she use her creativity, too. I'm sure she wouldn't want him spending more time at the office or on the golf course because he dreaded coming home. Long hugs, lots of patience, talking things through, and seeking to understand one another's feelings relieves a lot of stress. I call it "getting the wrinkles out." It's such a relief to connect, share together, and work things out so each person feels cherished.

The Delivery Room

If you have read books and attended classes with your wife, you will probably do just fine in the delivery room. Ask for a tour if one is offered. Of course, you can't witness *another* woman's birth, but it helps to see where things are likely to take place.

Most men tell me that the most precious thing on earth is to be present with their spouse and to help that wee one be brought forth into the living and breathing world. She will love you for your support. If you need a break, step out for a few minutes. It can be an overwhelming experience, one some men are not prepared for. Most men do just fine, but be sure to take care of you. Believe it or not, a few decades ago, men were not allowed in the delivery room. I'm glad we have come such a long way.

New moms experience pain and discomfort from episiotomy stitches, C–sections, tender or even bleeding breasts from nursing, and a host of other things besides hormones. It's no wonder they swear never to have another baby; yet after a few months, most women forget all the pain and discomfort and want to do it again because of the great pleasures of having children—and sharing that beautiful experience with their husbands. It is vitally important for you to be sensitive to all that she has been through and will go through for at least the first several weeks.

Money Matters

It's totally realistic to be concerned about money. Lots of couples delay having a child until they think they have enough money. Since there is never sufficient money, many couples end up never having children. I'm not saying you don't need to be prudent. However, let me warn you that you will probably never think you have enough, so if you really want a family, you will need to create a reasonable new budget that will include having children and all the expenses that come later.

Perhaps you will have to sell your motorcycle or your fabulous new sports car with that $500–a–month payment. Make some tradeoffs, because it will be totally worth everything you save to bring a child or children into the world. If you truly want children, you can make it work. Just know that the area of money is one of the biggest stressors in marriage, so develop a plan regarding your budget and spending/saving habits.

Will the Baby Change Our Relationship?

Hopefully, having a baby will make you closer and stronger; but it really depends on your desire, determination, and goals for your family. She's not a mind–reader any more than you, so tell her your feelings. Some of the communication tools will probably help a lot.

Here's a common scenario that came from Jeffery:

"I don't know what to do. I feel so guilty because I envy the baby. I love him dearly, but my wife spends all her time with him. I know he needs her, but I feel so left out, so alone, so unimportant. I know it's illogical, but I honestly feel rejected. I hope she'll want to make love pretty darn soon, as it's been weeks now, and I miss the woman I fell in love with."

And I said:

"Your feelings are absolutely normal, Jeffery. I understand. However, I can guarantee that things will get better. Make sure she has healed from giving birth before making suggestions about sex. You can snuggle and do other things to be intimate, you know. Just understand that the hormonal changes are huge and will take some time to return to normal. In the meantime, be patient. Ask her to include you in spending time with the baby, and request some alone time with him, too. Be open about your feelings in a loving way. You might say something like this:

'Sweetheart, I know you are exhausted with all there is to do for the baby and our family. You know I love him and am so happy he is in our lives. At the same time, I love you with all my heart, and I really miss being together. I really need more time and

closeness with you, so what can we do to make that happen? I don't want US to slip away.'"

I call this type of conversation "The Truth Sandwich." You can find more details about it and other communication skills in Chapter IX.

Men and Romance

Many men are very romantic, especially at the beginning of a relationship, while other men don't want to *admit* that they are romantic because they feel too vulnerable. This is a hard one for women to understand, but it's what some men have reported. Being romantic may not seem manly enough; and once he has done that, he has opened himself up to being rejected.

At the same time, men want to experience physical love and yearn to connect with their sweetheart. Though they may call it something else, they want to romance their woman and want her to romance them. If you ask, most women will tell you they love men who are romantic.

So just consider what you need and want and don't be afraid to talk about it. If you hide, hold back, or stuff your feelings, the resentment will build up, and getting back to a safe and loving place will be more difficult.

Will I Be a Good Dad?

This is really up to you. Being proactive, asking for what you need and want, being involved, and caring for her and your child are all things that will contribute toward you being an outstanding dad. Fatherhood, once taken on, is for always. It doesn't stop at birth. Am I saying the obvious? Gather information, read books, listen to CDs, etc. Later on, the two of you can go to a parenting class.

Spend time with your child or children. Remember, love is spelled TIME, and that goes for fathers, too. If your father was a good role model, follow his lead. If not, find other first-rate role models. Be interested in your kids, care about them, set good boundaries, and have a balance between a "firm spine and a soft belly," as described in a well-known parenting class called "Parenting with Love and Logic." In other words, be strong and clarify boundaries while also being kind and loving.

As I have explained, you and your spouse will be partners well after your children are grown, so make every effort to keep your marriage relationship close, intimate, and alive. Remember, the best gift you can give your child is a good marriage.

Just continue to be the awesome person you are!

His heritage to his children wasn't words or possessions, but an unspoken treasure, the treasure of his example as a man and a father.
—Will Rogers, Jr.

Options for Action

- Discuss how you can keep the bedroom a safe haven for relaxing and romancing, even with the baby present.
- Expect her lowered sexual desire, but do not underestimate her need for closeness and romance. Share with her your desires for closeness, even if making love is not possible for a while.
- Never underestimate the importance of being a father. Be proactive. Don't take a back seat willingly.
- Involve yourself as much as possible, both with her and the baby.
- Dream about ways you want to participate with your child as he or she grows up.
- Implement good self–care strategies. You will have more of what it takes to care for your loved ones.
- Be willing to get up in the night, help with chores, and be a good husband.
- Discuss a budget so that you can plan for those extra expenses.
- Make intimacy a priority. Modify as necessary, but be respectful.
- Keep communication flowing. Find out what's going on with each other. Ask for what you need and want, and ask her what she needs and wants.
- Say "I love you" every day. Words go a long way, as do actions. Give daily compliments.
- Spend alone time with your spouse as often as possible after the baby/children are in bed.

Chapter V
The Components of a Loving, Romantic, and Satisfying Marriage— After Children Arrive

When you like a flower, you pluck it. When you love a flower, you water it daily.
—Buddha

I think this quote by Buddha (Siddhartha Gautama, founder of the Buddhist religion) is good advice about how to create and maintain a good marriage and a happy home for your family. So how can it be applied to your spouse and children?

If you love someone, you will continuously provide "water" and nurturing to that person. You will delight in watching them grow. You will enjoy considering how much you can *give* rather than how much you can *get*. Watering your spouse can include being romantic, because adding romance is an important element to enhancing love. Certainly, children and babies can benefit greatly from loving attention, concern, and spending time together. With many of these things in place, you can have a beautiful and glorious garden.

Tilling the Soil and Growing Your Love

Marriage is like a garden. It must be tended to, watered, maintained, and weeded in order to be fruitful and productive. Obviously, watering is just one part of the formula, but if you love and take special care of all the *flowers* in your family, you will have a beautiful garden of joy and promise.

Weeds must be removed or they will choke both your relationship and family. They can take over the garden if they are not cleared out. Overspending, holding things inside, being critical, lustful thoughts, pride, and selfishness are just a few of the weeds that can flourish. So do your best to get rid of the problem areas before they escalate and compromise your happiness.

Here is a good formula for keeping love flowing through your marriage and family, and cultivating it like a garden of love.

Commit With Caring Hearts

Most couples love each other deeply when they get married, and they expect to live together for a lifetime. Few get married with the idea that they will one day end up divorced. Hopefully, you are in love with one another and have the basis for a caring and devoted relationship. If so, your two caring hearts will be invested in staying together, and you will be committed to caring for your children, too.

Merge Into One

Part of marriage is turning yourselves as two individuals into another entity in which you truly merge into one, just as the nutrients of the soil merge with the plants. This requires letting go of selfish, egocentric desires and meeting the needs and wants of your loved ones.

At the same time, you do not want to give up yourself as an individual. It is a delicate balance—caring for your own needs while also being a loving partner and parent. If you don't care for yourself, you may come to resent your spouse and your children through no one's fault but your own. It's important to continue to develop your talents and do some of the things you want to do whenever you can. Get someone to help you if you can't figure it out alone, and do not give up being who you are.

Add an Abundance of Love

My friend Melissa related a sweet story about a lovely moment between two of her friends who had just had a baby.

Vickie and Todd's baby was about two months old when Melissa took a baby gift to their home. Vickie was outside on the patio dressed in her bathrobe. Her hair was tousled; she had no makeup on and certainly wasn't looking like a beauty queen. The baby was nuzzled up to her breast having his lunchtime feeding when Todd came home for his lunch. He looked at his wife and baby and said, "Sweetheart, I've never seen you look more beautiful than you look right now."

Melissa was tearful as she told me about this experience. Hearing it was very touching to me, as well. Todd created both a loving and romantic experience simply because he was so in love with Vickie and their baby. What a fortunate wife and baby to have such a loving husband and father.

There are so many ways to add romance to your love life, so be imaginative. Verbal expressions, opening her door, sweet little surprises like a note under her plate, a heart with a love message on his mirror in the bathroom, or a call in the middle of the day inviting him out lunch can add richly to your love and romance. I suppose we could say romance is in the eye of the beholder. So make an effort to learn what is meaningful to your partner and do that.

Cultivate Respect and Trust

Respect in marriage means that people trust and support one another. They are willing to understand, give acknowledgment and validation, and value each other's wishes, opinions, and independence. They give the benefit of the doubt and choose to think in positive terms about one another. When insults, name–calling, sarcasm, or put–downs are given, they create hurt and pain. At that point, respect is in jeopardy. Certainly, differences can be resolved, but that should be done with understanding and positive regard. If respect is not present, it will be difficult or impossible to weed out the negativity or resolve issues. It is equally important to cultivate respect and trust with your children.

Trust is the feeling of being able to rely upon another's honesty, integrity, and truthfulness while having confidence in their words and deeds. People *earn* our trust out in the world, but in marriage we want to believe that our partner is trustworthy. Little white lies can escalate into betrayal, secrets, disloyalty, and even infidelity. This creates distrust that is very difficult to repair. Without mutual trust, a relationship can go into a destructive mode very quickly.

Share Gentleness, Laughter, Hope, and Joy

These elements are pretty self–explanatory. A touch of gentleness and laughter can mitigate many potential hazards, just as fertilizer helps a garden grow.

Hope means having a desire or an aspiration. It is easy to have hope, but without meaningful action, it will just be hope—something wished for but not attained. When you know what you hope or wish for, you need to take the steps leading you in a direction to reach that goal. Sometimes, when we feel like quitting, hope says, "Never give up."

Hope is being able to see that there is light despite all of the darkness.
—Desmond Tutu

Joy and humor go a long way toward creating happiness. Sometimes, joking about an issue can take away stress and allow you to save face or formulate a change without making a big deal of things. However, coarse, sarcastic, or hurtful humor is never effective and only serves to cause harm and distance. Use words and actions that provide support, offer encouragement, and are uplifting. A joyful heart is a gift to both the giver and the receiver.

Deliver Understanding

Most of the time, people think that in order to identify with someone, they have to be in agreement. That is not true. If it were, there would be little understanding toward anyone about anything, because few of us think the same way about everything. Understanding means to perceive the meaning of or to comprehend what another is expressing. It has nothing to do with agreement or acceptance.

I once heard an interview between a couple. The husband was a devout Democrat, and the wife was a devout Republican. Obviously, they rarely, if ever, agreed on politics. For a fight to ensue, they reported that both people needed to be involved. If one of them chose not to engage, the discussion would go nowhere. In political matters, they rarely agreed and knew they would be unsuccessful in changing the other's mind. So they just either agreed to disagree or said, "I really don't want to argue about this." They respected one another enough to drop the subject. Sometimes a useful strategy in creating harmony is simply "agreeing to disagree."

Show Affection

Most people enjoy tokens of affection such as small touches, hugs, and gentle kisses of the hand. Holding your sweetheart's cheek and looking into her eyes says "I love you" and conveys that feeling as much as anything else. If your partner doesn't like overt displays of affection, find out what *is* meaningful. Is it the written word? Is it phone calls? Is it sharing what has happened during the day? Is it emotional support? On the other hand, if you are the one who doesn't like affection, perhaps you can explore the reasons why and work on it, because touch in a relationship keeps it vibrant.

Touch is the first sense babies acquire. Loving touch leads to healthy physical, emotional, and mental development and helps to create a strong sense of self. Children who are loved, hugged, and touched grow up to be more loving and affectionate, too, because they feel better about who they are.

Nurture and Water for a Lifetime

Alice, the wife in a dear couple I knew, told me this when they had celebrated over 50 years of marriage:

Many times, we seriously considered getting a divorce. But we honestly couldn't afford it, so we just stayed put. We are so glad we stayed together, unhappy as we were for a while, because we ended up working out the kinks and becoming best friends and lovers. I can't imagine our lives without each other.

Whether in a first–time marriage or a later one, older people can have fun, play, be intimate, have sex, and feel great closeness, too. Many couples have endured hardships; but it is always gratifying to see loving partnerships that have lasted 50, 60, or even 70 years or more.

Thriving in the Garden of Love

Put all of these concepts together and you have the formula for a contented couple and a happy family.

Commit with caring hearts. Merge into one.
Add an abundance of love. Cultivate respect and trust.
Share gentleness, laughter, hope, and joy.
Deliver understanding. Show affection.
Nurture and water for a lifetime,
And you will thrive in the garden of love...
And have a beautiful family, too.

Marriages, like a garden, take time to grow. But the harvest is rich unto those who patiently and tenderly care for the ground.
—Darlene Schach

Everyone Has Problems

It is important to remember that every marriage has issues as well as challenges. If you have problems, it doesn't necessarily mean you have a bad or unhappy marriage. Nor does it mean you don't love or care about each other, though it may feel like it in the moment. It just means that sometimes you may experience struggles, strains, and adversities.

When people are stressed or overly tired, they are less patient and understanding. Quarrels are more likely to erupt. But if individuals can maintain respect and kindness even in their disagreements, serious damage won't be done to the relationship. They can resolve things constructively rather than destructively.

Evelyn and Howard, a newly married couple I saw, were having some rather significant struggles. They argued about having children, something they should have discussed before ever getting married. They quarreled about spending time with Howard's friends, some of whom Evelyn did not like; and they were in disagreement about how much time to spend with one another's families. The constant bickering caused them to wonder if they were compatible.

The two of them were contemplating separation but were curious to know why some people stay together despite problems and why some choose to divorce. While there is no simple answer, I gave them the formula for a happy marriage and told them that it was a good starting point. I also said that some couples had simply made a commitment to work things through no matter what (unless, of course, the issues were of an unresolvable nature). As we negotiated the bigger matters, the smaller ones fell into place, and they saw the value of thriving in the garden of love. They were able to give up their selfish ways and water the seeds of their love.

Working Things Out

It seems to me that every girl/woman wants to be treated like a queen, and every boy/man wants to be treated like a king. Wouldn't life be beautiful if we could keep those concepts in mind when relating to our partner? If these are in place, closeness, romance, and love can thrive (in addition to a few other concepts). If they are not present, intimacy, romance, and even love may be missing, and the relationship may be in jeopardy. When you seek to understand one another's perspectives and viewpoints in a respectful manner, you will enjoy spending time together. Often, when you do so, the "problems" will disappear.

Kelly and Tom had a fight every Sunday before they went to dinner at Kelly's parents' home. Tom would rant and rave and make excuses about why he couldn't or didn't want to go. Usually he went with her but held a lot of resentment. Kelly accused him of not liking her family and denying her the opportunity to see them.

In therapy, as we worked to discover the real issue, they learned to listen to each other with an effort to understand. They realized that Tom very much liked Kelly's parents, but he just wanted some time at home on Sunday afternoons to watch a game or take Kelly to a movie. The resolution simply involved staying at home at least every other Sunday and being open to discussing whether it worked for both of them. Tom respected Kelly's need to be with her family, and she respected Tom's need to do other things on some of the Sundays. They were both willing to compromise their desires in favor of the relationship.

In close relationships, what is often neglected is a willingness to bring up difficult topics in the first place. Some individuals stuff their feelings or go along with someone just to keep the peace. They fear it is of no use to bring up certain subjects, and so they avoid being honest. However, if feelings are submerged, they can escalate to a point where an explosion occurs and the matter gets very heated. Resentments build, and the relationship can suffer.

Anger is often avoided, but it is a real and important feeling. If you look at my model for anger in Chapter IX, you will see that there are layers to anger. When those are discovered, it is easier to bring up sensitive topics to relieve stress so that things are not said and done that are later regretted. When you learn to use effective communication, you will gain confidence that it is safe to discuss almost anything.

Sometimes we make things up in our heads and don't discern the difference between reality—what is really going on—vs. the stories we create in our minds

The Platinum Rule

People have long tried to live by the Golden Rule, which says, "Treat others as *you* want to be treated." It has its purpose and often serves us well. But have you heard of the Platinum Rule? It says, "Treat others the way *they* want to be treated." Which phrase sounds more caring of others? You can shift the focus from "I'll give people what I want" to "Let me understand what they want so I can give that to them." Use the Platinum Rule, and you might be amazed.

Here is an example of my husband's loving care for me as he has delightfully warmed my heart, as well as my hands and toes. To me these were very romantic gestures offered out of pure and unselfish love. What could be more romantic than that? He gave from his heart a precious gift I will always remember with joy and gratitude. That's just the way he is!

One morning, after a big snowstorm, I kissed my husband goodbye before I left for my office. As I began scraping my car windows, he came dashing outside and took the scraper from my hand. When I realized what he was doing, I said, "Sweetie, I'm fine. Please go inside. You'll catch your death of cold." But he persuaded me to get into the car so he could continue his efforts. Then he noticed I had forgotten my gloves, so he ran inside and got them.

Later, he called to say he had inadvertently kept my scraper. Yup, the sweet guy brought it to my office, because the snow hadn't subsided.

Commitment

Without commitment, it is easy to be attracted to another new or exciting person, toss up your hands when the going gets a bit rough, or simply exist as roommates. Many couples who stay together have made a firm commitment to love and cherish one another, remain loyal, and make their relationship a priority. They are diligent at working things through even if they have had problems.

Some couples have made a religious commitment before God that they strongly feel compelled to keep. Those who do not have a religious belief and have not encountered serious issues—such as addiction, abuse, adultery, or other grave matters—frequently entertain that same strong commitment. Others have experienced financial difficulties, problems with a child or loved one, a debilitating illness, or other significant matters; but it is their commitment and deep love that have kept them together. That is why I am very passionate about helping people develop a strong foundation, so that when unforeseen circumstances occur, they have the tools to get through the difficulties.

When children come into a family, parents have an obligation to do all they can to work things out before deciding to separate. While I'm not saying that people should stay in a miserably unhappy or dysfunctional marriage just for the sake of the children, many people give up too easily, without endeavoring to repair their broken relationship. In such cases, children are usually the biggest losers—unless, of course, there are abuses or other critical problems. Obviously, all the tools in the world cannot make someone love another individual or keep the commitments once made; but those who are committed and loving toward one another have something that is beyond anything money can buy.

> *People stay married because they want to, not because the doors are locked.*
> —Paul Newman

Forgiveness

Living without regrets is a beautiful way to live. This is not always possible, but if there are things you regret, ask for forgiveness. My daughter once said, "If my husband were to die tomorrow, I'd know we have had a remarkable life together. We have never waited for a great life to happen, because we aim toward creating it every day."

In addition to asking for forgiveness, another key is being willing to forgive rather than holding onto offenses. Letting go creates peace; and don't most of us want more peace? An apology goes a long way. Everyone does things they regret. It is also important not only to forgive your partner but to forgive yourself. Of course this involves the ability to talk things through with respect rather than blame.

A friend of mine recently told me that a few years ago, she and her husband used to fight a lot. When they couldn't resolve an issue, they would sometimes go for days without talking to each other. Often, her husband would storm out of the house, come home late, and sleep on the couch. He wasn't out drinking or carousing; sometimes he just went to a movie or restaurant to simmer down.

On one of these angry escapes, he got into a car accident with a drunk driver. When they realized that they could lose one another in a flash, they decided (the operative word here was *decided*) that their way of handling their disagreements wasn't working. Their relationship was too precious, so they found some good books and learned how to talk about things in a calm manner rather than quarrelling, blaming, or stuffing their feelings. Their pact was very successful, and now, even several years later, they get along very well.

If Something Works, Do More of It

I always ask couples I see in counseling to describe what caused them to fall in love and choose to be together. This way they have an opportunity to recall the positive attributes and experiences they had early on. I also ask them to express what has been working well instead of focusing on what is wrong. This will assist their efforts to continue doing things that make them stronger. Of course we address their disputes and disagreements and work to resolve them, but I think it is important to *"catch* their spouse (or children) doing something good." Unfortunately, when upsets fill the air, people frequently fail to see that there *are* things that are going well.

A very effective concept is, "If something is working, do more of it. If it isn't, do something different." Now, that seems simple enough, but frequently people get stuck in old patterns. They don't even entertain the idea that they could do something on their own to alter ineffective behaviors and attempt something new. Maybe he is tired of his wife always being grouchy. Changing his behavior could be as simple as remembering to thank her for each delicious meal she prepares, or following through on something he promised to do. She might remember to tell him how handsome he is or thank him sincerely for an act she appreciates. Gratitude, appreciation, and compliments can go a long way toward creating a happy environment.

A college freshman was having a personality struggle with one of her roommates. She decided to think about and write down all the positive qualities of her friend, and then she recounted some of them to her. Here's what she wrote about her insights:

> *We all need positive reinforcement....People don't know what we are thinking unless we tell them. So let's let the people we love know that we are thinking good things about them. Recall a relationship that means a lot to you; it could be with a brother, sister, spouse, grandma, daughter, friend, etc. Take the time to either write them a letter or talk to them in person and share the qualities that you admire in them. It can make all the difference....When I told my friend the things I admired, she was very appreciative. It totally changed our relationship for the better and became an important lesson for me.*

Time Together

Couples often tell me they don't have time to talk, time to date, or time to be together. I don't buy this argument at all, because even the busiest person can find time for things they want to do. Spending time together is a matter of desire, priorities, and planning.

Not wanting to be together is a different situation altogether and may need some intervention or repair. If you don't spend time together, how can you communicate, enjoy the present, or work on the matters that are most important to fix?

Create ways to spend *quality* time together with simple, routine activities. Even with children around, you can eat, snuggle, fix dinner, flirt, play a game, go for walks with the baby, or watch a movie while sitting on the living room floor. It doesn't always have to involve money.

Dating is Not Optional

One of the best things you can do for your marriage is to have regular date nights. These are essential, not optional. Too many couples get so busy that they don't take time for one another as a couple. It's even more challenging with a baby or little ones, but it can be done with extra effort and careful planning. Create the time, find a sitter, and do things together on a regular basis.

When Brad and Helene saw me for counseling, they hadn't been out alone together in over six months. They felt distant, lonely, overwhelmed, and "uncoupled," as they called it. None of their family lived in town, and they didn't trust anyone to watch the baby and three-year-old son. I suggested that they call neighbors to recommend possible babysitters.

They found Izzie, a fifteen-year-old who babysat for their best friends. I made two suggestions: First, I submitted that they could have her come to the house when Helene was there to observe how things felt. Secondly, when they were comfortable, they could leave for an hour or so and see how things went. I also suggested that on their dates, they were not to talk about any issues or problems, but were to act as they did when they were dating in college.

The first time Izzie came, Helene just stayed in the spare bedroom and did some drawing that she had not touched for years. She also observed Izzie and developed enough confidence that she and Brad planned an evening out for ice cream. Since that worked out well, the next week they went to a movie. A couple of weeks later, they felt relaxed enough to go out for dinner and a movie. Yes, it was an expensive evening, but they reported that they talked about goals and plans for their lives; they even got a bit flirty and sexy. What a difference just being together alone made to their marriage.

Plan your dates to be once a week, or no less than twice a month. Even if you just throw a blanket on the floor, watch a movie, and eat popcorn, you can consider it a date and make the time special. Don't discuss problem areas; just have fun. A weekly planning meeting is also beneficial, but do not combine it with your date night. Date nights are for having fun and just connecting in an enjoyable way.

It is also imperative to teach your children that Mom and Dad need alone time. It just takes a bit of preparation. You can even lock the bedroom door for some intimate time, as long as the baby/children are safe. I'm sure you can find ways to nurture yourselves once you realize that time together is critically important. If you want a good relationship, *dating is not optional!*

Accepting Each Other

You don't need someone to complete you. You only need someone to accept you completely.
—Unknown

Acceptance of one another is a principal feature of a successful relationship. We could go into all the many differences between men and women, but the bottom line is that we are different. The sexes are obviously distinctive, and we all have quirks and traits that we might want to change in ourselves or another. Acceptance recognizes and values ourselves and others for who we/they truly are.

If we find certain attributes to be undesirable, we have several options: manipulate, criticize, retaliate, negotiate, commit to the relationship no matter what, or leave. Feeling accepted means we are certain we are loved and embraced even when disagreements occur. This makes it easier to resolve difficulties. If changes need to be made and there are love, respect, heartful negotiation, communication, and a strong commitment, a firm platform will exist whereon people *want* to make changes for the sake of the relationship.

A few years ago, one of my clients came with her husband to a marriage workshop I gave. At the time, their marriage was in some real trouble. Later, she told me that counseling and the workshop had given them a great many tools which they were both willing to use.

"We learned to accept each other's differences, which are many. Of course it takes work. But we have gained an appreciation of each other for the various roles we play and have learned to express thanks and gratitude…. People communicate differently. My husband became very tense when we needed to discuss something the least bit controversial. I have always been more verbal, wanting to resolve things quickly. However, I began to stuff my feelings so as not to upset him, but that just made me more resentful.

"I learned to read his body language and facial expressions in order to decide when to talk. When he was tense and tired was NOT a good time. Since he couldn't read my mind, I had to be more direct with him in my requests. Being able to calm myself and slow down helped a lot. Then he was more able to share himself with me. I know these things seem simple, but when you're upset, they're the last things you think to do. We really love each other and are so grateful for the tools we acquired and implemented."

When your attitude is, "I choose to do things for you regardless of what you do or don't do for me," then you will complete words and actions out of desire, not obligation. If pervasive selfishness exists on the other side, things may not work so well. Patience and time may be required, even counseling.

In any case, acceptance will go a long way toward creating positive changes. You got together for some sound reasons, or you wouldn't have picked each other. Review what brought you together in the first place, and see if you can rehabilitate those things that were endearing, compatible, and joyful.

> *Success in marriage does not come merely through finding the right mate, but through being the right mate.*
> —Barnett R. Brickner

One Individual Can Change the Relationship

One individual's actions can totally change a dynamic. If one partner isn't invested in making things better, complains of being too busy, is too upset, or seems unwilling to look at his or her part, that person alone can negatively affect interactions. Conversely, doing only one or two simple things the other partner values can change the situation for the better. It may not happen overnight, but I have seen it happen successfully time after time. Persistence in doing effective acts will pay off.

> *Becca's husband frequently came home tired and depressed from a day at work. She immediately wanted to "pounce" on him, telling him that the baby cried all day, how she couldn't get anything done, and that their two–year–old dumped and smashed a whole box of graham crackers on the floor. Frank was usually grumpy and upset and screamed at her to leave him alone and give him some peace and quiet. Becca felt terrible and came to dread his coming home. Their arguments became more prevalent and radiated out to lots of issues. She tried to get him to go to counseling, but he refused, saying it was all her fault.*

Feeling desperate, she came to see me by herself. She learned that she could impact Frank's reactions by her actions alone, and we made a plan. After one of our sessions, she asked him to sit down and describe what he desired from her in order for there to be more peace. He said he was exhausted when he came home and needed time to unwind. All he wanted was about 20 minutes to relax and rest before interacting with the family. The next evening when he arrived, Becca gave him a kiss and hug and suggested he take some time to himself. In addition, she made sure their two–year–old was doing something quiet and the baby was already fed.

As she implemented these strategies, Frank was much more relaxed and engaging when he rejoined the family. She was affectionate, asked about his day, and simply gave him an opportunity to talk about himself or whatever he wanted. Sometimes she told him about her day; but the nice thing was that after she left him alone, he was actually interested in what had happened for her and also asked what she needed from him. Without her openness and curiosity, he might never have asked the question. She replied that when he came home, all she needed was a hug and a kiss and that she would gladly give him the time he needed. She was happy to share the day's events later, when he was more rested. As a result, they grew closer and enjoyed their time together.

Becca was able to impact the marriage simply by suggesting they talk together, giving Frank an opportunity to express himself, creating a relaxed atmosphere, and being more affectionate and interested in him. The final shock for her was that he said he would be willing to go to counseling if she really wanted to go. By then, she didn't even find it necessary. What a change in their lives!

Wishing Time Away

Some folks seem to want things to happen immediately, or even yesterday. *"I can't wait until*...the baby sleeps all night, I'm done with diapers, Joey can walk, James goes to school, winter is gone, my husband gets a better job, I lose weight." It's called wishing time away—or wanting better times ahead. While it's tempting to worry about difficult stretches and anticipate the future, it is best to be fully engaged and enjoy the precious present. The years go by so quickly, and each event is meaningful, even the struggles, for in struggling we reshape ourselves and our relationships.

Take Care of Yourself

The ability to love others is based largely upon the ability to love oneself. If your parents, teachers, or others were harsh, full of unrealistic expectations, or gave you negative messages, your self-worth may have been terribly diminished. In an effort to be loved, you learned to meet the needs and desires of others. You may have conformed, complied, tried to do things right, and learned it was best not to cause trouble. This became such a habit that you had difficulty respecting or even knowing your own needs and wants.

Katrina was a pleaser. From her perspective, her parents were loving as long as she did everything they wanted. When she didn't serve their desires, she was either punished or they became withdrawn and distant. She had been taught to comply with others' wishes so much that as an adult, she couldn't love or care for herself. As she continued living up to everyone else's expectations, catering to her family, serving in church and school, and giving her best to her husband, she had little time and energy left for herself. As a result of her upbringing, she didn't even recognize what she herself wanted and frequently became drained, exhausted, and resentful.

When you over–give, resentments can prevail, even though they may be hidden from your awareness. They can appear in many ways, such as confrontation, manipulation, or sarcasm. So it is vital to take care of yourself. If you do not, you will be unable to serve others in the ways you desire. Your bucket needs to be filled, too.

I know this has been said before, but it bears repeating. In your marriage, save out some parts for yourself. Take care of your own needs, develop your talents, and do some of those things you want to do without giving up who you are. I have seen too many individuals, especially women, relinquish doing things they desire for the sake of the relationship. Later on, they come to resent their spouse or/and their children, which is not very fair. Each person desires and deserves autonomy. I know it's difficult, but you must do it or you will come to have hard feelings for your family, which does not create happiness for anyone.

Friendship in Marriage

Friendship is a key ingredient in a loving relationship. Friendship means sharing hopes and dreams, likes and dislikes, discussing future goals, knowing one another intimately, and caring about one another's welfare. Many of my acquaintances who have been married a long while say that being best friends is at the core of their marriage. Statistics bear this out as well.

They love, honor, and respect each other's desires and wishes, share intimacy and romance, and support one another. Their firm *commitment* creates the binding cord for their lasting marriage. Friendship enriches love, which enriches commitment, which enriches friendship, and so forth.

Unfortunately, some women disclose intimate topics with friends or family members and have little need to share with their mate.

When I began seeing Isabelle, she spoke of being best friends with her neighbor Gayle. They would get together almost daily and let their kids play while they talked about all the things that bothered them. Isabelle shared with Gayle her unhappiness with her husband and got lots of sympathy. Gayle also had numerous gripes and complaints about her husband and discussed her goal of going back to college when the kids were older.

Because they shared so much, they didn't talk much with their husbands. They grumbled and complained so much to each other that they failed to work things out with the people who really mattered. You can imagine that both marriages suffered.

As Isabelle began to recognize her role in her marital unhappiness, she distanced herself from Gayle's complaints and began sharing more with her husband. As they engaged in joint counseling to iron out some of the problems, their happiness returned, and they grew very close to one another again. On the other hand, once Gayle no longer had Isabelle as a sounding board, she chose another route. She moved out and essentially left her husband and children to pursue her own goals.

It's fine to have a good friend, but let your spouse be your *best* friend. If he or she isn't your "bestie," consider what you need to do to change the dynamic. It's up to you!

A friend is one who knows you and loves you just the same.
—Elbert Hubbard

Make Your Relationship the Priority

Imagine a big umbrella or canopy over the two of you with a sign that says: "Our relationship is more important than ___ (wanting to be right, getting my own way, spending money the way I want, buying a new motorcycle without consulting my partner, giving all my attention to the kids, etc.)." Fill in the blank as it applies to you.

A good way to show that your relationship is your priority is to be aware of your partner's needs and wants. There are few things people truly need, but the word is still viable because it can be used as a gentle request. Simply ask your sweetheart how you can meet his or her needs. Be clear and specific in your response, such as: "I need (or would like) you to be more physically affectionate," or "I need (or would love) for us to talk about the dreams we have for our family." Then do your best to meet those needs and desires.

Rewards come when you radiate love, give your relationship the time and effort it deserves, have regular date nights, create romantic moments, compliment each other, give long hugs, express appreciation, confer about important decisions, and show genuine interest in whatever is going on with each of you.

Above all, don't forget about your kids. They want mom and dad to stay together. Make your relationship a priority— not only for yourselves, but for your precious family.

A truly successful marriage is one in which each partner has total complete confidence in their mate to have their best interests at heart.
—Chaim Bentorah, God's Love for Us: A Hebrew Teacher Explores the Heart of God through the Marriage Relationship

Options for Action

- Discuss how to make your relationship the main priority so that your child/children will have a happy and secure family.
- Examine how you can implement the Platinum Rule, and do more of what your partner would like.
- Evaluate you past dating practices, and decide how you can date on a regular basis.
- Rate your level of friendship at this time from 1–10, with 10 being the best. Discuss how you can improve that number as needed.
- Notice how happy couples and families behave with each other as you are out and about. Write down and share your thoughts.
- Change up your wardrobe so that you are not always wearing grungy casuals. Wear snappy, sassy, or sexy casuals even when having that "date" at home. Look your best even when you don't feel like it.
- Evaluate the words and behaviors that are most effective in your relationship, and work to do more of those things and less of what isn't effective.
- Write down *your* family formula for keeping your marriage loving, romantic, and strong.
- Ponder some things you can do by yourself to change something about your relationship.
- When out in public, find a special signal to show love, such as a wink, air kiss, or special smile.
- Create a mood and pull out one of your most romantic ideas.

Chapter VI
Intimacy and Sexual Expression

Those who have never known the deep intimacy and the intense companionship of mutual love have missed the best thing that life has to give.
—Bertrand Russell

Intimacy means knowing someone deeply and sharing the most private and personal things of life with them. It is an emotional state generally reserved for the person to whom you feel closest. You are each able to let down your guard and share your inner worlds. Making love is only one expression of intimacy. Words are often unnecessary because your hearts are so harmonious. You can share the whole gamut of feelings, including sadness and pain, as well as joy and exhilaration. Adding romantic actions only adds to the magic of love and intimacy.

Parents' Love Affects Children

When children see their parents showing love, affection, and talking about their lives and their family, it gives them a sense of safety and security. They are aware that Mom and Dad care for each other and that love and harmony abide. In fact, the deep intimacy their parents share may even permeate outside of the bedroom (without them hearing or knowing the details, of course) and influence their lives in meaningful ways.

Phyllis' parents quarreled a lot. No affection was shown, no fun was had, and they bickered constantly. She feared almost every day of her young life that her parents would divorce. That led to deep insecurity and fear, but it also affected her self–esteem well into her adulthood. Only a lot of counseling helped her understand that she was a valuable person. Children often believe that they are the cause of their parents' unhappiness, which is certainly not the case.

Jessica's parents, on the other hand, teased, hugged, and shared their love for each other and their children on a daily basis. This assured her that she was valued and loved and that her parents would remain together. She felt safe and secure in the arms of her family; and as an adult, her confidence and self–esteem flourished.

These examples illustrate how important your relationship is to your children. It can affect their entire lives in either positive or negative respects.

The Meaning of Intimacy

In a loving relationship, intimacy creates meaningful sexual expression, and meaningful sexual expression builds intimacy. Together they become a beautiful circle of love. Sex is a physical thing, while intimacy is much more.

Engaging in sexual intimacy demonstrates love and caring as well as showing a willingness to both give and receive pleasure. It fosters closeness and facilitates feelings of connection physically, emotionally, and spiritually. Most of us have a desire for love, commitment, affection, and nurturing.

Unless there are extenuating circumstances, sexual expression is the delightful glue that binds a good relationship. However, that may not be possible if a person has just given birth, is ill, paralyzed, or has some other situation where they cannot make love.

Intimacy can be created without sexual expression through various types of loving exchanges: talking, sharing deeply, going on dates, reading together, offering massages, sharing interests, praying together, enjoying family togetherness, and much more. Whether there is sex or not, love, respect, commitment, compassion, and consideration of a partner's needs, desires, and pleasures are vital.

Intimacy means different things to different people. To one person, it means receiving hugs when she is cooking dinner, a tender look of love and admiration, carrying a heavy grocery bag, holding hands on the couch, preparing dinner together, or a back massage. To another person, it means being acknowledged for something nice he did to help, a surprise picnic after work, a hug and thank you while he washes the dishes, sexual teases while he is working in the garage, or most certainly sexual activity. So find out what creates feelings of romance and intimacy in your partner and do those things often.

The Reasons for Sex

Obviously, there are many reasons for sex and sexual intimacy. Of course, the most beautiful one is when it expresses love, closeness, and togetherness to those who deeply love each other.

A few others are for physical fulfillment and enjoyment, gratification, stress relief, and a need for affection and attention. Today's habit of "hooking up" for casual sex between those who are simply strangers or brief acquaintances is admittedly done simply for emotional or sexual gratification, no strings attached.

The most foundational reason for sex is that it keeps civilization going through procreation. I heard of one instance where a person expressed the idea that "couples get pregnant just to create little images of themselves." Sounds pretty demeaning, doesn't it?

If sex is constantly pushed upon someone, or it is more than they can handle, they may become resentful, experience stress, or feel like a sexual object. Such pressure, especially if the refusal is met with anger or hostility, is extremely off–putting; and it may take a while before the approached partner wants to be physical again. Pushing or forcing sex is not conducive to a loving and close partnership. Good relationships require compromise, discussion, and negotiation so both people feel valued.

The common assumption is that men need and desire sex more frequently than women. However, some men have a lower sex drive than women.

In most cases, if it feels obligatory or mechanical, or that it's done as a favor, it is unsatisfying. Wayne Dyer said, "Relationships based on obligation lack dignity." When sexual expression is performed as a chore or a gift without mutual sharing of love, it may provide a physical outlet but not be very meaningful; and over time, damage can be done to the partnership or/and the individual.

Rose discovered that whenever Ben was grumpy, he needed or wanted a sexual release. "Every time we got together, his mood improved and he'd be back to his kind, sweet self. I used to make love to 'help him feel better,' but that wasn't satisfying for me. So I changed my attitude. Now we get together often because of our love, not out of need. We both feel loved and cherished, and so our lovemaking is more passionate, frequent, and romantic now. I believe it was possible because I altered my responses."

False Expectations

Hardly anyone tells you that the insatiable and thrilling honeymoon–stage sex drive won't last forever. It simply doesn't, which can be a huge disappointment. Those tingling, tantalizing feelings eventually diminish. On a joyful note, as a compatible and committed couple ages, their love can grow deeper and more profound.

You can have truly beautiful and sexual experiences that increase over time when you love each other deeply— and, I might add, when you keep things "exciting." Surprise and novelty are quite powerful and can keep boredom and complacency at bay. So if you aren't already doing so, explore this concept and enjoy your intimate life together!

Why Making Love Is So Important in a Marriage

Sexual intimacy with someone you love promotes closeness, connection, comfort, relaxation, and so many other good things. Though certainly not the most important element of a marriage, it can be one of the most beautiful, satisfying, and unifying of all activities. When it is missing, people can feel distant, hurt, rejected, and unloved.

Emotional closeness creates passion. Without emotional closeness, sexual contact can be physically satisfying, but it lacks passion and can feel empty to those who desire connection. Sexual desire includes both physiology and emotion. Keeping romance alive involves exploring and finding ways that say "I love you" in a way that is appreciated and well received.

I have counseled several couples in which sex was pretty much non–existent. It can work if both parties are in agreement; but if one of the partners wants sex and the other doesn't, the relationship can deteriorate, closeness may decrease, and anger and resentment will come in its place.

> *Joel said, "When I reach out to my wife and she says—as she frequently does—that she is too tired or is not in the mood, I feel unloved and terribly lonely. She's not there for me anymore, and it makes me not want to be there for her. After a while, I feel angry and resentful and give up even trying. I can't stand the rejection much longer."*

Sexual Challenges

A large study of sexual satisfaction in long–term relationships showed that those who were most satisfied were able to communicate about their sex lives. They talked about their needs, desires, likes, and dislikes, and were happier in their relationships. Mood–setting, foreplay, variety, frequency, and communication were some of the important predictors of satisfaction.

Some couples find it extremely challenging to discuss sexual desires, needs, and wants. Sometimes, reading a book about sex can make it more comfortable and will lead to personal discussions. Another idea is to just explore each other's bodies through sensual touch and gentle massage of many body parts, not allowing it to lead to intercourse.

Through sounds and words, you just might find out what is pleasurable and lessen the discomfort of talking. During the day, you can use sexual teasing, suggestive comments, or anticipation for the night's activity. Of course, if it is convenient, it's fun to be sexual at any time day or night. Above all, say the words "I love you" frequently.

Whether making love or simply pleasuring one another, it is important to provide feedback. Let your partner know when something is satisfying—again, through sounds and words. If something doesn't work for you, express it in a kind manner. Never, ever demean your partner.

Because of childhood wounds, rape, or physical or emotional abuse, making love can be troublesome for some individuals. Even when one feels completely sexless, perhaps because of a physical or psychological problem or erectile dysfunction, there are solutions. Certain medications may detract from sexual feelings on the one hand, and, on the other, there are several medications, herbs, and other solutions that can help. If there are physiological problems—some of which may be caused by pain, medications, alcohol, mood disorders, body image, stress, or other difficulties—help is available from a doctor, counselor, or sex therapist. Michele Weiner Davis, in her book *The Sex–Starved Marriage*, has a lot of valuable suggestions on this topic.

Sex and Pregnancy

We've already mentioned how a woman's sex drive often decreases during pregnancy. However, during pregnancy, some women experience a *heightened* desire for sexual activity. For example, my client Susan reported having an unusually high sex drive at that time. She wanted her husband even more than he could handle. Wouldn't most men love such a challenge? However, after giving birth to her baby, she had no sexual desire whatsoever. He was definitely deflated by her drastic change of heart.

Another client, Laura, had no desire for sexual intimacy during her pregnancy. "It's all I can do to get up in the morning. By the end of the day, after taking care of the chores and our two–year–old, I have nothing left." While I understood what she was saying, because I remembered my own four pregnancies, I urged her to set aside her lack of desire, at least some of the time, to consider her husband's needs. As she was able to increase her ability to put her husband before herself once in a while, he became more responsive to her needs. When she made sexual advances toward him he was, of course, ecstatic—and it gave him hope for future intimacy.

I reminded him that her situation was temporary—although no one could know exactly how temporary. I proposed that he attempt to meet her needs while being as understanding as possible. She claimed she needed more help with housework and wanted him to comfort her when she felt sad and overwhelmed. When he began doing more of those things and also displaying greater understanding for what she was experiencing, she felt closer to him. As they learned to discuss their wants and desires, their relationship dramatically improved.

Sometimes these differences can be very disconcerting. People often wonder why the sexes are so different. But as Yoda said, "There is no Why, only Do." It is just the way it is, and individuals ought to do their best to make adjustments. Understanding and awareness can be cultivated.

Why Sex After Childbirth Might Be Challenging

I have mentioned some of the challenges previously, and a few others are listed below. More than anything else, it is important to discuss all of your concerns openly. If you don't, misinterpretations, resentments, feelings of abandonment, and other misunderstandings can create significant obstacles to your closeness. Some of your concerns and worries may be similar, but you won't know unless you talk about them. So share your feelings and let each other know what is going on. Only by keeping the lines of communication open and kind can you work through issues which arise.

During the first few weeks or months after childbirth, intercourse may cause pain or even tearing. Bleeding should have stopped, but the perineum needs to heal before a woman will feel comfortable. It also takes time for healing to occur from a C-section. If either one of you is anxious or tense, you won't become aroused. There are plenty of things you can do with and for each other to keep the love lights burning. So have fun!

- Getting pregnant again too quickly can be a huge fear. Nursing is definitely not a fool-proof form of contraception, as so many have learned. So use something you have confidence in if you don't want to get pregnant again right away.

- Moms often may not be able to relax, especially if the baby is in the bedroom with you (which I think is wise to accept for a while). She will feel the need to give the baby her undivided attention, especially if she is nursing. It's also more convenient for dads who provide help. As I've said, making love may not be her top priority for a time.
- Again, fatigue, lack of sleep, discomfort, etc. are prevalent. Just remember, do your best not to take these as rejections. They are very real. Discuss them and continue to be loving toward each other even so.
- Some inhibitions may occur and attitudes may change as a result of childbirth. Lower your expectations but do discuss your feelings.
- Babies and children seem to wake up or need attention at the most inopportune moments. Also, spontaneity can become more challenging. So make the most of your opportunities as they arise, since they might be fleeting.
- Take things slowly. Enjoy each other without expectations. Cuddle and be emotionally intimate. If you are touching and kissing along the way, returning to actual sex will feel less daunting. If you are not intimate during this "down time," it may be challenging to be sexual later on.
- Massage is a great relaxer. However, the downside, especially for men, is that besides being relaxing, it can be sexually arousing.

Libido

Obviously, there are often significant differences in sexual desires and libido between men and women. A major reason is chemistry. Testosterone, one of the hormones connected to a man's sex drive, is usually 20–40% more prevalent in men than in women; therefore, his sex drive is commonly stronger. Medications can be useful if that hormone is lacking.

Another difference in libido is that generally most *women* have a need to feel an emotional connection *before* they want to be intimate. She wants to spend time together and engage in meaningful communication where she feels heard, understood, and respected. She also wants her partner to share in the burdens of housework and caring for the children. If these needs are met, she may be more willing and desirous of being sexual. If they are not met, she may feel abandoned, angry, or distant leading to—you guessed it—no sex.

It's no surprise that *men* usually have the flip side at play. But, of course! Why are we so opposite? Generally speaking, most men tend to feel close and intimate *after* the sexual act. In addition, they have a need to feel close before doing chores and other acts she desires. So, in essence, if he is not getting his needs met, he may not want to spend time with her or communicate in the way she needs; nor will he feel like sharing the chores, rubbing her sore feet, or getting up in the night with a crying child.

The reverse may be true in some marriages. In my practice, I have seen several women who are frustrated by their husband's lack of sexual interest. More common, however, it is women who think men are merely oversexed. "Every time we snuggle, I feel like a pocket knife is in my back," said one of my clients quite disparagingly. She obviously didn't want sex as much as her husband.

Guys didn't ask to be this way. His sexual responses are often automatic and unintentional. Be glad he is turned on by YOU and not by someone else. Yes, it may feel tedious at times, when you just want to snuggle without anything else, but at least take his interest in YOU as a compliment.

Many women who are uninterested in sex simply *refuse.* As I've said, this can be exceedingly harmful to a relationship. Unfortunately, some women don't seem to understand that one of the secrets of keeping their husbands close to them is through sexual fulfillment. They will be more relaxed, more present, and feeling more devoted when this important need is met. On the other hand, husbands should respect their wives' desires, interests, and body concerns and be willing to meet them halfway, which means *not always* giving in to the sexual urge.

Frankly, you do not have to be in the mood or feel sexually aroused before making love. Sometimes, all it takes is starting the process. Things fall into place, and you get into it even when you weren't to begin with. Sometimes it's important to "just do it." The willingness to both give and receive pleasure is at the heart of intimacy. A good marriage involves meeting in the middle, compromising, respecting one another, and sharing willingly. So give your hearts as well as your bodies.

Differences Between Men and Women

Did you know that there are significant differences between men's and women's *brains*? It's no shock that at times we feel worlds apart, as though we came from different planets; but the fact that the brain itself is involved is a surprise to many. The differences are, of course, generalizations, since there are always exceptions. At the same time, it should be remembered that no one way of doing things is better or worse than another.

It is not my purpose here to go into detail about the physiology of the brain, but it is interesting that Dr. Gregory L. Jantz, in the February 27, 2014 issue of *Psychology Today*, reported that the categories of differences are in the areas of processing, chemistry, structure, blood flow, and brain activity. These show up in our relationships, communication patterns, language, emotions, stress levels, spatial abilities, mathematical skills, sexual appetites, susceptibility to brain disorders, and other matters.

Small Changes, Big Results

Most men admit they need a physical release, but they also say that closeness, intimacy, nurturing, validation, and comfort are even more needed. Most men give liberally when they are loved and nourished.

So, ladies, if your guy isn't giving to you, what can *you* do? Take responsibility for your part and do something to make a change. If each person gives at least 75%, the bases are covered, right? Even if you believe that your part is only 10%, consider doing what you can to fix things on your own. Of course, the reverse is true as well.

Sylvia felt she was losing touch with her husband and that he was becoming more and more distant. We talked about her giving him a heartfelt hug and kiss when he left for work and upon coming home. She also left a few love messages on his phone and under his pillow. Above all, she stopped telling him about all the things he wasn't doing. Soon, she noticed that he was calling her from work, and sometimes he asked her out to lunch. From that point on, their relationship began to improve simply because she had changed by giving extra love and adding sweet, romantic touches.

So you see, one person's small changes can yield big results. This next change in a couple I was counseling was quite remarkable.

When Jane and Ronald came for counseling, their marriage was in real trouble. They were angry and frustrated with one another and hadn't made love in over a year. After a couple of sessions of dealing with issues, they admitted they had no idea how to make the first overture toward making love, even if they wanted to, which they didn't.

At our next session, I suggested they start by giving each other foot and hand rubs, no sex allowed. I also recommended that they spend time talking about some of the fun and loving times they had previously experienced. At our next session, they reported they enjoyed their time together and felt more connected. They even found themselves a bit turned on but followed my instructions and didn't pursue their urges. This was a hopeful sign, because their sexual feelings had all but turned off.

The next week, I suggested they give each other gentle massages with some sweet-scented oils and talk about what they each relished most in bed. Oh, my. They couldn't stop themselves and gave in to lovemaking. All the built-up stress, anger, and resentment dissipated. We were then able to work on a few problems that they confessed were pretty unimportant in the overall scheme of things. After that, their relationship improved.

Making Love Is Not a Spectator Sport

A lot of couples use the excuse that they don't have time for each other because of the children. Really? You are the parents. You should be in charge. I know that it is difficult with a baby and toddlers, but do your best. With older children, have family time from 6:00 to 8:00, or whatever fits with your work and the kids' bedtime schedules. But after 8:00 or 9:00, let the children know this is *your* time—the hours for the two of you. Children, even teenagers, need 9–10 hours' sleep every night. They need to at least be in their rooms and leave the two of you alone, unless they have special needs such as being ill or upset.

You need to *claim* time to talk, read, watch a movie, go to bed early, and just *be*. If you don't set firm rules around this, children will take advantage. Yes, your rules will be broken at times, but let that be the exception rather than the norm. And how about *you* getting together in the bedroom instead of watching someone on TV or in a movie? If you don't want to be together, something may be off in your relationship and you need to fix it!

Sexual Intimacy Around Children

Some people wonder if they should engage in sexual intimacy around their baby. I have found no studies to suggest otherwise. The following are my personal recommendations.

If a new baby is sleeping in the room with you, I see no problem in being sexual. They are too young to be aware of what you are doing. However, I would be careful not to do anything that might be very loud or perceived as threatening. Babies receive impressions even in utero if parents are fighting or if a mother is severely emotional. They are even more vulnerable outside the womb, and certain sounds may seem frightening to them. In order for parents to have utmost freedom of expression, I personally think it is best for babies to be in their own rooms as soon as they are not waking up for frequent feedings. Of course, it is your choice.

It is important for children of all ages to see you being affectionate. It provides them with healthy role models and helps them feel safe and secure in their family. As a general rule, avoid being sexual in front of a child who is over six months or so.

Is your child in bed with you? I'm not talking about a baby. There is nothing wrong with this, except that it keeps you as spouses from connecting emotionally and physically, and it makes real communication challenging. In addition, it can create your child's dependency on you for comfort. You need time alone; so let them come to bed with you in the morning or for special times. You be the judge, but just know that it may keep you and your spouse from activities that foster your connection.

Another problem is letting children stay up late. Again, it impedes your time together. Sometimes this can be an *excuse* for avoiding each other, which may be the real issue—not the children, the TV, or other distractions. If your "tire is flat," fix it.

How Often Should We Make Love?

It isn't the number of times people make love that is most important. It's about caring, valuing, and feeling bonded with one another. One of the ways to do this is by picturing what it's like to feel the way the other person feels—imaginarily walking in their shoes for a time. When people feel understood and appreciated, they are more likely to be responsive to the needs of their partner. So be sexual sometimes even when you don't feel like it. Once you get started, it can be enjoyable and mutually gratifying. It merely takes beginning. It's best if each of you is willing to both initiate and respond. Either person can make overtures. Just be respectful—and have fun!

Care of the Body

Newlyweds can quickly gain ten to twenty pounds because they enjoy going out to dinner and cooking delicious meals and desserts. But in pregnancy, weight gain is inevitable as well as advisable. The baby needs nutrients, and so Mom must keep her body well–nourished with a balanced diet.

Most doctors advise a woman of average weight to gain 25 to 35 pounds during pregnancy. Underweight women could gain up to 40 pounds, and overweight women only need to gain 15 to 25 pounds. Even so, it's much easier if you stick to the lower end of the ranges, because those extra gained pounds are difficult to lose; and as we age, it gets harder and harder. Stay in touch with your doctor for your specific needs and those of your baby.

The best time to take off weight is as soon as possible after childbirth. Be diligent about diet, sleep, and exercise. Eat plenty of protein, and be sure to get lots of fiber found in vegetables, fruits, and whole grains. Watch your intake of bad fats. Our bodies need fat, so consume healthy fats such as nuts, seeds, and vegetable oils such as coconut or olive oil. Too much sugar is also unhealthy, and so is an abundance of refined carbohydrates, like breads, white rice, and pastas.

Stay as stress–free as possible, though that's hard with a new baby. Get plenty of sleep and as much exercise (strength training is excellent and efficient) as feasible. Green tea is known to boost metabolism, and lots of water is very important, especially when nursing.

Beauty is not in the face; beauty is a light in the heart.
—Kahlil Gibran

Most people don't like to hear this, but there is frequently a correlation between physical attractiveness and loss of desire. I'm talking about after the baby has come and you are back to normal. Though it may seem shallow, sexual desire can diminish because a person has put on lots of extra pounds or their grooming or cleanliness has been neglected. That goes for men as well as women. It's a known fact that outer beauty and attractiveness keep one appealing to their partner. So, each of you should have a goal to stay healthy, desirable, and physically fit.

> Paul told me, "Peggy was a beautiful girl when we got married. But after the baby came, she seemed to lose interest in herself. I know she was exhausted, but she really let herself go. Sometimes she doesn't even comb her hair in the morning, and putting on makeup is a thing of the past. She looks good when she goes out with friends or to church, but around me—well, I hate to say it, but she's been frumpy for over three years, now, and has gained about 40 pounds.
>
> "I've talked and talked to her about it. I've even given her new makeup and clothes, and I've provided money for a weight loss program. But she just doesn't get that I feel closer to her when she makes an effort to look nice for me. It feels like she doesn't care. She even said to me once, 'Why can't you just love me for me, just the way I am?' That was tough. She's my sweetheart, and I don't want to lose interest, but I'm starting to feel differently about her, and it breaks my heart."

For both of you, a healthy diet, cleanliness, neatness, good grooming, exercise, and decent apparel all contribute to feelings of well–being. It makes most people feel good to take a shower in the morning, fix their hair, and consider what to wear, even if they are just staying at home. These elements are also important for keeping romance alive, because appearance is either attractive or not. It is natural for individuals to be drawn to appealing, beautiful, and nice–looking persons, places, and things.

Obviously, beauty is more than skin–deep. Inner beauty and desirability lie within and are composed of many things: humility, kindness, humor, intelligence, courage, self–acceptance, caring, accepting others for who they are, being present when needed, smiling, forgiving, telling others what you appreciate, radiating love, and so much more. It's not just about looks. However, the body is a beautiful thing, and you owe it to yourself and your partner, whether male or female, to care for it diligently.

> *True beauty in a woman is reflected in her soul. It is the caring that she lovingly gives, the passion that she knows.*
> —Audrey Hepburn

Keeping Love Fresh in Later Years

You may be saying, "The later years? We are just at the stage of having children!" I get that, but I want to talk about the future for a minute. What about your love, romance, and intimacy after you have been together for 5, 10, 20, 30 years or more? How do you keep your love and romance fresh and alive?

I hope you will find your way. But I can say that if you allow your relationship to get old, routine, uninteresting, or boring, you are heading for trouble. As people get used to each other, they get into routines that are unproductive for intimacy and sexual expression. So I'm just giving you a valuable suggestion: Keep things fun and interesting.

He may stay up later than she does watching TV, working on the computer, or playing video games. She may write emails, read a book, or spend an hour on Facebook. They do their own separate things and are disconnected before going to sleep. And then they say, "We never have time to talk or be together." Really? Maybe they're just avoiding each other. While these activities are fine on their own, the danger is that if the habits are not suspended from time to time, people get set in their ways and their love life declines. You can be together if you want to and if you make it a priority.

Perhaps when he sees her reading, he doesn't want to interrupt her, even though he feels sexual. Or she feels sexual, but he's watching a football game. By the way, a TV in the bedroom, as well as doing work in that room, can kill romance like nothing else. Think about saving the bedroom for talking (not arguing), reading, doing something together, lovemaking, and sleeping.

Plan your schedule so you can often *go to bed at the same time*, talk, and take love signals seriously. If you develop a good relationship in the beginning, rich with love and romance, as well as habits of spending time together, your later years will have a better chance of being fun, special, and full of romantic interludes. Yes, it takes thought, preparation, and even spontaneity, but it can be luscious.

This is an experience of a woman who had been married to her soulmate for 30 years:

> *"As I stood at the stove, he came up behind me and wrapped his arms around my body. 'I'm so happy to be married to you. You have made my life complete. I don't know what I would do without you.' He is such a sweetheart, and we have been so happy. He has healed my heart and blessed my life and the*

lives of our family. I am so fortunate to have him and can't imagine existing without him."

Inner Beauty

If your relationship is built on good looks, lust, sexual pleasures, and doing things your own way, the chances of an enduring relationship are small. Realistically, bodies age, hormones change, muscles ache, breasts droop, wrinkles arrive, and "stuff happens." But if you value your marriage and make it a priority, you will commit to meeting each other's desires, both sexually and non-sexually, for many years to come.

While caring for the body is essential and remaining attractive is prudent, the *inside* of a person is most important and lasting. Physical beauty is transient, but inner beauty lasts forever. Yes, inner beauty is the real jewel of a person and shows up when you are true to yourself, feel good about who you are, treat others with care and respect, provide loving service, and let your inner light shine. So let your light shine!

People are like stained–glass windows. They sparkle and shine when the sun is out, but when the darkness sets in, their true beauty is revealed only if there is a light from within.
—Elisabeth Kübler–Ross

Options for Action

- Discuss ways you can increase your intimacy. Even if making love is not possible, discuss ways to give one another pleasure.
- Engage in physical closeness and making love, even when you don't feel like it.
- Talk about sexual needs by asking your partner what he or she would like you to do to make things the most satisfying.
- Give compliments liberally: "Your body is beautiful." "I love those stretch marks because they mean..." "Thank you for helping with the baby last night. I was so tired."
- Talk about the differences in your libido and what to do about it. Make accommodations to please one another. Do what works, and do it often.
- Make a routine meal into a special dinner for two after the kids are settled down. Flirt with each other. Show affection. Sexually tease.
- Change up your wardrobe so that you are not always wearing grungy casuals around the house. Wear snappy, sassy, or sexy casuals even when having that "date" at home. Look your best even when you don't feel like it.
- Prepare a warm bubble bath for both of you with a lighted candle in the room
- Plan a date night and get the sitter.
- Put a surprise package together, the way kids do in high school when asking for a date. Ask a teen for some fun ideas.
- Give 10–second hugs instead of a passing wave or non-acknowledgment.
- Plan a surprise getaway for a few hours, such as going for a look at the fall leaves, a picnic in the park, or a bike ride. Or pack his/her suitcase and don't say where you are going.

Chapter VII
Typical Causes of Stress
During Pregnancy and After Birth

Do not assume that differences doom a marriage. It's disrespect for the differences that doom the relationship.
—Anonymous

Why am I focusing so much on challenges? Well, it may be because many couples don't do well, at least for weeks, months, or even years after a child is born. Because of so many changes and stressors along the way, life can get a bit off track. Unfortunately, during this time, a few spouses lose their commitment to the relationship. This is sad indeed. But if you know it's not easy and that by hanging in there life will get better, perhaps you will be more willing to develop patience and understanding and have greater concern for your partner.

Many couples get through the tough periods early on and have problems later. One client told me, "I think the later years are more challenging than the early ones with kids. I wish I'd had the knowledge back then about some of the things you're writing about." It's all a matter of your own circumstances, perspectives, and behaviors.

Children Are Not the Cause of an Unhappy Marriage

According to the Gottman Relationship Institute, within three years of their child's birth, about 70% of couples experience a significant slump in their relationship quality. Do you suppose it could be because there is so much unpredictability and unknown territory? I think so. That's why information is so valuable!

Perhaps I'm restating the obvious, but no matter what is going on, *children are never the cause of adult issues.* There is no question that they can complicate our lives, but they are not the *cause* of our human struggles, conflicts, dissatisfactions, or differences. Some parents erroneously blame the children because they don't want to take responsibility for themselves; and oftentimes children carry guilt for their parents' foibles. Let's remember: It's not the challenges that cause problems; it's how people handle them. How couples treat one another is the secret to satisfaction and happiness.

> *Being in control of your life and having realistic expectations about your day–to–day challenges are the keys to stress management, which is perhaps the most important ingredient for living a happy, healthy, and rewarding life.*
> —Marilu Henner

A Pattern That Could Develop

So what causes an unhappy marriage? There is no one answer that fits all. For right now, the focus is on having a baby, so if this isn't you, at least you can see the typical pattern I have witnessed over and over during my personal and professional experiences:

- **They** (the couple) feel very excited about the birth of their new baby. Their pride in each other is awesome, and their joy is abundant.
- **She** becomes overwhelmed, getting up so much during the night and doing all she has to do for baby/children. She's exhausted and gives all her attention to the baby and little if any to her husband.
- **He** starts to feel alone, abandoned, and no longer cared about. He becomes jealous of her time with the baby; he feels despondent, neglected, and even depressed.
- **She** doesn't understand his feelings because she believes she is giving everything to everybody and has nothing left.
- **They** bicker and quarrel. Effective and loving communication is minimal.
- **He** feels even more abandoned and retreats more and more. Since she seems uninterested in being intimate, he starts to doubt her love.
- **She** feels alone, unattractive, and unloved.
- **He** retreats even more. Sex is a distant memory.
- **She** doesn't feel supported and her irritation builds.
- **He** focuses more on himself, his work, sports, friends, the computer, etc.
- **She** becomes angry and resentful because he's not helping with all there is to do and is not being her companion.
- **He** distances himself even further.
- **She** starts to believe he doesn't love her and becomes more distant, irritable, and hostile.
- **He** stops giving even more. His anger and resentment increase. He gives up on sex altogether because he has been refused far too often.

- **They** argue more and spend little time with each other except to take care of the necessities.
- **They** don't communicate their feelings, and each one is locked in resentment and ineffectively expressed or unexpressed anger, which come out passive–aggressively.
- **The relationship** is in jeopardy. Both are miserably unhappy.

WHEW, what an awful scenario. I'm exhausted just thinking about it! Unfortunately, many have experienced parts of this cycle and have found it to be most unpleasant and debilitating. If this has happened or is happening to you, reread pertinent sections and keep reading for more ideas. What follows are just a few possible causes of unhappiness.

> *Happily ever after is not a fairy tale. It's a choice.*
> —Fawn Weaver

He May Not Be Able to See Her as a Sexual Lover

One phenomenon, though uncommon, is that some men have difficulty seeing their wives as lovers. They almost put them on a Virgin Mary–type pedestal. My client Thomas said, "I feel guilty making love to my wife. It almost seems sinful to be passionate with the goddess who is carrying our child." I know this may sound over the top, but it does happen.

A few men are actually turned off by the physical changes in their wives. This is a rare occurrence, and such feelings may not last long. If there is not a change of heart, it does not bode well for the relationship.

She Doesn't Feel like a Sexual Person

When she was single, she felt beautiful, desirable, and sexy. But *now*? Forget it. She feels like a big, fat balloon. Sexual thoughts can be nonexistent. In addition, although it may be unconscious, she sees her main role now as Mother, not Wife and Lover. Of course, this is not a healthy scenario. If you are not being a good and loving partner as well as a good and loving parent, your child will suffer the consequences. So keep the romance alive by making each other important despite the needs of the baby and/or other children. And do *not* neglect one another.

Depression and Baby Blues

Depression can beset anyone at any time, both men and women. Some depressions are serious or clinical, while most are situational. When the tough situation passes, so does the depressed mood. Of course, hormonal changes can exacerbate any circumstance and cause things to look bleak. This is disconcerting. But medication, counseling, and good communication might be of great assistance. Please note: A doctor must monitor medications very closely during pregnancy and during nursing, or the baby can suffer side effects.

Baby blues in moms are common after childbirth, but are usually mild and last only a few days to a few weeks. Some characteristics are mood swings, sadness, anxiety, overwhelm, crying spells, loss of appetite, and/or trouble sleeping. The symptoms are not severe and usually don't require treatment.

Post–Partum Depression

Though not common, post–partum depression occurs in some new mothers and is considered a serious illness. It is characterized by deep sadness, hopelessness, and feelings of worthlessness. It can begin anytime within the first year after childbirth. The mother may have trouble caring for and bonding with the baby. Severe symptoms include thoughts of hurting the baby or herself, and she may have little or no interest in the baby. Treatment should be sought immediately. Symptoms can last quite a while and really must be treated by a doctor and/or therapist.

Most children don't have specific memories of events until they are at least three years old, but they do receive impressions of love, warmth, and caring or the negative opposites. All these early experiences form imprints that can last a lifetime. However, during this difficult period, a loving and caring spouse, family member, or caregiver can provide the nurturing the baby needs. So do not despair. With the right help, the symptoms will hopefully not be lengthy.

She's Not Sure She Will Ever Have Her Life Back

When my oldest daughter was near full term with her third child, I tended my two grandsons while she went on a business trip with her husband. One afternoon, she called, sobbing. "I'll never get to go on another trip after the baby comes. My freedom is almost gone." She didn't even enjoy her vacation because she was so worried about never being able to go again. Of course, that didn't occur. Over the years, she has been able to go on many trips.

Plans just need to be made in advance. Now that her four children are married and are having their own babies, she jumps in to help them whenever she can. And she's had lots of vacations!

Family members are great helpers; just be sure you don't overwork them. So are friends and neighbors, if you can work out trades. A teen, or even a pre–teen, can give you a break. You could stay home and take a nap, read a book, knit a scarf, or plant your tomatoes. If you have other children, let them help. Even a young child can fetch a diaper or a low–lying bottle.

It's Up to Both of You to Keep the Romance Alive

Sometimes moms forget the importance of being a wife and lover, and dads simply give up and take a backseat with hopeless surrender. This is not a good option for either one if they want a strong marriage with tenderness, kindheartedness, and adoration.

If she spends most of her time with her child or children and leaves her husband to fend for himself, she might wonder, *Why is he so unhappy? Everything's fine for me.* But after a while, when he gets used to dealing with things on his own, she becomes lonely and miserable and has no clue how the deterioration occurred. If she doesn't make the relationship a priority, he may feel unwanted, depressed, undesirable, and unattractive. And if he doesn't express what's going on with him or make an effort to be with her, she will feel abandoned, too. So keeping the lines of communication open is critical.

Disagreements

Many partners share common ideals, goals, and purposes for their lives, which leads to appreciating one another more fervently. They want to work to keep their lives harmonious for the sake of the family.

However, everyone has disagreements, because no two people are wired the same and no one has a perfect clone. Each individual desires to have a certain amount of autonomy and control, express their own opinions, and do things as they wish. And yet, in loving relationships, negotiation and compromise are necessary for peace and harmony to exist.

One thing is for certain: Nothing is ever solved when people are angry. Each person has a need to be heard and understood, and that won't happen when people are overwrought with anger. So wait until you can both be calm, and then express your feelings. Create a safe space for your partner to express themselves as well. Try not to sweat the small stuff, and be patient. Remember that most likely you both desire to have harmony and a peaceful relationship. So find your commonalities—what you can agree upon—and go from there with respect.

Above all, don't let your distress and resentments build up. Otherwise the pressure cooker is likely to explode. Keep your frustrations on the table and learn to communicate wisely and kindly so as to nip in the bud matters that can escalate.

Differing Parenting Styles Can Lead to Trouble

For many, after the glow has worn off and the sleepless nights and fatigue set in, the stresses become enormous. But after the baby grows and matures, other issues can erupt. Marital discord can happen, especially when individuals have different views regarding rules, discipline, leniency vs. strictness, attention–giving, bedtimes, priorities, friendships, and so many other issues.

If you are not on the same page in your parenting, life can become complicated and dissonant. Children learn to manipulate the two of you. And you may have ongoing arguments about the same issues.

In addition, your own lives get more complicated as children age. Juggling housekeeping, grocery shopping, exercise, PTA, home repairs, maintenance, employment, play dates, ballet lessons, soccer team practices, birthday parties, family visits, and so forth becomes daunting as well as exhausting. I can't stress enough that you must talk and decide together how you want to manage these matters. If you do not, you risk constant disagreements and potential disaster.

Charles and Rose had been married for five years when they decided to have children. They came in for counseling when Charles was at a breaking point with the marriage, while Rose wanted to save it. At the time, Thomas was 10 and Millie was 12. Charles reported that he was quite strict with them but was also kind and communicative. He expected a lot but explained things so they understood the rules, and he spent quality time with them. In fact, he said the three of them had a great relationship.

Rose's parenting style was more lenient, and the children manipulated her often when Charles wasn't around. He came to believe that she spoiled them dreadfully. He also said she was more interested in her family of origin and her work than in spending time with the children. Often she would let him "represent" her when the children had activities and she wanted to do something else. He became frustrated and started distancing from her. She in turn felt discounted and alone. It became a cycle of indifference and separation for both of them.

They reported that the first five years were wonderful together. In looking back, they admitted that their problems began after the children came on the scene. The spontaneity, sexual intimacy, and time spent together took a backseat to the children. When they tried to talk, they both became defensive and the conversations went nowhere. So the problems festered for years without resolution. They thought about counseling but never followed through.

They rarely went out together, and when they did, the children complained and wanted everyone to be together. In fact, the couple had been on only one trip, just the two of them, since Millie was born. To decrease tension and arguing, they stayed home or did things with the kids. Gradually, Charles and Rose began spending less and less time together. They went to bed at different times and had totally different interests. Needless to say, the closeness they had once experienced was gone, truly gone.

This is an important illustration, because it exemplifies some of the challenges that keep couples from connecting and remaining intimate. It can happen so gradually that no one realizes what is happening. One partner may think things are just fine, while the other feels they cannot abide the situation any longer.

Parenting styles can absolutely get in the way of closeness. It is a topic most people don't take time to discuss before children come on the scene or even after. Unfortunately, many don't seek counseling or any kind of assistance until the fractures are so deep that they cannot be healed.

You *must* put time and energy into your relationship, or it will fail. You need to date, go off on weekends once in a while, and put the children to bed so you have time together—not working, texting, or playing solo computer games. Talking, sharing, laughing, and having fun are crucial. So are solving problems in your parenting and agreeing on values, rules, discipline—everything, really. But if you love and enjoy one another, and are able to negotiate disagreements, even the most challenging problems are easier to unscramble.

A Few Statistics

According to Divorcestatistics.org, the divorce rate for first marriages in the U.S. is 45–50%, for second marriages it's 60–67%, and for third marriages it's 70–73%. Forty percent of couples with children divorce. Though it is projected that the rate is decreasing, those statistics are still pretty staggering.

Some people give up quickly on their marriages and don't give them a chance. It is wise to wait until things settle down and life has a chance to resolve before making such a life–altering decision, because usually the situation will improve over time, when the stressors of having a new baby decrease.

Research also shows that the average age of people going through their first divorce is thirty. People at an older age have learned that many issues are temporary and *can* be resolved. But young people, especially if they haven't had good role models, don't know this fact and imagine that the only solution is to leave the relationship.

Divorce May Not Be the Answer

Today, our legal system allows couples to give up easily. Separation is often considered when couples drift apart, stressors get the best of them, negative patterns root in, and both spouses feel hopeless and helpless to turn things around. If one feels disrespected, ignored, or unloved over a period of time, he or she may decide not to remain in a loveless and uncaring marriage. Emotional or mental disorders can also cause serious strain on a relationship, especially if medications, counseling, or other help are refused

For over six years, I taught a court–ordered parenting class for divorcing parents. I designed my own course, which was called "Hope for Our Children." It was surprising to find that numerous couples had filed for divorce before the baby had even arrived, or soon thereafter. I'm sure many of these couples had rushed into marriage for some ill–founded reasons and hadn't known one another well enough to make such a life–altering decision. Others stayed married for a few years and then decided to give up on their marriage without a great deal of effort. Some had good reason, because of abusive behaviors, affairs, addictions, or other serious issues.

The worst part about divorce is that it is extremely difficult for children, regardless of their age. Here are some things kids have said about their parents' divorce:

> *"We didn't ask to be born. How do they think we will ever believe in love or marriage?"*
>
> *"Yeah, you can survive a divorce, but it makes you not trust yourself or anyone else. I'll always be afraid to get married."*
>
> *"It was like a wildfire. I had no idea it was coming. The pain and loss were almost unbearable."*
>
> *"Don't they get it? Why did they have us kids if they were just going to split up? They coulda just worked it out."*
>
> *"I just hate both of them. I thought we had a great family. Now I have to go back and forth, back and forth. I don't want to be with either of them. They are ruining my life."*

Obviously there are many viable reasons for dissolving a marriage. In a relationship that has experienced adultery (which can sometimes be worked through), physical or sexual violence, emotional abuse, serious addictive habits, intense ongoing anger, dishonesty, or criminal behaviors, divorce may be the most viable option and the only way for people to move forward.

Divorce is not something to be ashamed of; but if the relationship is salvageable, it is worthwhile to do everything possible to make it work, especially when children are involved. Couples who stay together and work through their difficulties have a tough task, but it is possible to end up happier than they had envisioned.

Sandra G. Bender, a psychotherapist, states: "Two-thirds of unhappily married adults who stayed married reported that they were happily married five years later." That is promising news.

It is my hope that individuals who are struggling will receive counseling and do their best toward making things better before jumping headlong in the direction of divorce. There are multitudinous remedies for those with a strong commitment to salvaging their marriage.

> *Coming together is a beginning; keeping together is progress; working together is success.*
> —Henry Ford

Options for Action

- Figure out how you can keep your relationship at the top of your priorities. Remember: "The best gift you can give your child is a happy marriage."
- Discuss the challenges and stressors in your lives. Do you need family help, hired help, greater understanding, or more effective communication?
- Discuss together and gather information to understand what's going on if one is depressed or unhappy.
- Mom, don't leave your husband out! The mother instinct comes in strongly, and if you take over and don't let him in, he will learn to stay scarce.
- Dad, keep involved with your wife and with your child/children. Communicate your needs, and recognize how important you are.
- Whenever you come home, greet one another with a hug and a 15–second kiss (no pecking allowed). Teach your children to make a fuss over each parent, too.
- Show love and affection in front of your children.
- Get away separately and give one another breaks.
- Write down ideas to get away together as much as you can, even if it's just for a few hours.
- Implement romantic and loving actions you have previously discussed.
- Make lovemaking special by doing something unexpected and showing that you think your partner is extraordinary. Words are important, too.

Chapter VIII
Other Challenges to Creating Romance in Parenthood

The future will present insurmountable problems—
only when we consider them insurmountable.
—Thomas S. Monson

Regardless of how much people hope to avoid adversity and heart–wrenching experiences, there are many life–and–death events that can challenge even the most caring of relationships. Trials, pain, and death are a part of living on this earth. Though they may seem insurmountable, most situations can be healed given time, adequate support, strength, and courage. Even the most influential and powerful people of the world, down to the most downtrodden individuals, have overcome debilitating obstacles that draw out qualities they never knew existed.

Expressions of grief and loss are typically profound and are intensely conveyed in order to cope with the situation. The effects on each person vary significantly.

Coping with the Challenges

Some of these challenges may be a miscarriage, a premature birth, sudden infant death syndrome (SIDS), birth complications, an abnormality, a disability, or some other tragedy. Any one of these can be devastating and may cause the family significant disruption.

When such things occur, some couples draw closer, while others become angry or distant. The emotional overwhelm is substantial and frequently affects the relationship in negative ways. Some individuals lay blame on their spouse, a doctor, or someone else and will hold onto their anger for an extended period of time.

It is important to recognize that there is no predictable time frame for recovery. Though this doesn't seem like much of an answer, *it takes as long as it takes*. Each person grieves in a different manner, so patience, love, and empathy are deeply needed. One person may need space and time alone, while another needs comfort and reassurance.

It is important to allow one another to grieve, talk, or cry as much as necessary. Deep anger, sadness, depression, and guilt are common. The situation may affect intimacy, finances, self–esteem, mood, parenting styles, and so much more.

Ask for what you need and want. Hopefully, your need will be understood, and it will be provided in a loving manner. It is critical to do everything in your power not to let these terrible experiences destroy your marriage. Utilize friends and family (but try not to wear them out), and find support groups and professional assistance as needed.

Though it may be difficult, those couples who join together with understanding, compassion, and support will get through the crisis. When both people are willing to make the relationship a priority and grow together to accept the realities, make a plan, and move forward, the marriage can not only survive, but beautifully thrive.

On the other hand, some couples cannot endure the intense grief and unexpected changes that come about.

They may quarrel, blame, shame, lose patience, or react in any number of unseemly ways. Sometimes a woman believes that her spouse is not as emotionally affected as she. Even if he doesn't express feelings outwardly—which is a tendency in some males—he is most likely suffering as much as she.

It is not uncommon for one parent to want the other to feel an equal amount of hurt, which sometimes leads to insults, sarcasm, accusations, or emotional withdrawal. The stress may be so strong that one person feels a need to escape. In some cases, divorce seems like the only solution. It is sad indeed when couples allow such challenges to destroy their relationship without at least giving time and effort toward healing.

Friends and family members, as well as spouses, may wish for a grieving person to be "normal" because they can't handle the upset, tears, or depressed mood. Please keep in mind that grief cannot be rushed, though time and counseling will help. Therefore, it is highly valued and appreciated when others show compassion, understanding, and support during such difficult periods. Asking for assistance from a spiritual leader, family member, or therapist can also afford much-needed aid.

Premature Birth

"Oh, my, our precious babe is no larger than Daddy's hand. He's stuck in an incubator, and we can't bear to leave him." This scenario creates tremendous pain and stress for a family. It is heartbreaking not to be with your newborn until he is healthy enough to come home. Babies require emotional love and physical touch, which is often problematic when a baby is being protected in a snug and safe environment, possibly with tubes and monitors galore. Most hospitals allow parents to hold and cuddle their baby. Sometimes, volunteers provide this caring service, but the best scenario is for family members to be present as often as possible.

When my second child was born, it was I who had to stay in the hospital for an extra five and a half weeks with blood clot complications. I missed my three–year–old daughter Theresa and baby son Charles Robert terribly. They were not allowed in the hospital until I was almost ready to come home (although my husband sneaked Theresa into the room once—with a nurse's collaboration). It was very tough to have missed those precious weeks with both of them. Thank goodness for my mother and sister–in–law, who were there to help my husband.

Death of a Child

The death of a newborn, an infant, or a baby with sudden infant death syndrome (SIDS) is shattering and can cause heartbreak like nothing else. Parents have the expectation that their child will live a good life, well in excess of their own. They believe that's the way it's supposed to be. Sadly, not always. When a child dies, it denotes the loss of all future hopes and dreams for that loved one. I can hardly imagine that kind of pain. Certainly, it results in sorrow of great magnitude.

The mother who has carried a child inside her for many months is especially affected, but it is devastating for the father and other family members, as well. The youngster who has been expecting the arrival of a baby brother or sister is usually miserably disappointed. They can hardly comprehend death, anyway. Though healing will occur, such grief can be a lifelong and painful process. It can be beneficial for the whole family to find ways to honor and preserve the memory of the lost child, such as planting a tree, or creating a shelf or wall for memorabilia. Certain people want to never speak of the incident again. Truly, that is not a healthy thing to do.

Death at any age is traumatic. I recently counseled a family who lost an eight–year–old girl. An illness came upon her suddenly, and the doctors could not diagnose the problem until it was too late. She is survived by her parents and her twelve–year–old sister. You can only imagine this family's desolation, as well as that of other family members, friends, classmates, teachers, teammates, and sports coaches. She was dearly loved.

Babies and Colic

Colic is the term used to describe excessive and uncontrollable crying in an otherwise healthy baby. Many babies experience colic at two to three weeks, but it is usually short–lived. Fortunately, colic causes no harm, except to parents, who feel they are losing their sanity. Often, there is no consolation for the crying. A doctor should be consulted to exclude more serious conditions.

Colic doesn't cause gas in the tummy, but more gas can be created because the baby swallows more air when he cries. Overfeeding, undiluted juices, food allergies, and emotional stress can aggravate the situation. It will pass, but assistance from family members or others can help to relieve the parents' tensions.

Physical or Mental Impairment

When a child is born with a birth defect or other physical or mental impairments, it can be grueling for families. Some problems include Down Syndrome, Autism, Asperger's, Rett Syndrome, Childhood Disintegrative Disorder, Cystic Fibrosis, Cerebral Palsy, Spina Bifida, Fetal Alcohol Syndrome, and others. Professional support is usually essential for the child, as well as the parents and others in the family. Of course, disabilities and deficiencies may happen to any family member at any time.

Attention Deficit Disorder (ADD), Attention Deficit with Hyperactivity (ADHD)

These diagnoses can be exceptionally frustrating and challenging. However, specialists are immensely helpful. Many children outgrow ADD or ADHD, while others struggle through adulthood. In some instances, it isn't diagnosed until later years, even into adulthood. Drugs can be useful, but I can't urge you enough to seek professional assistance. Do everything else possible before utilizing drugs. Setting up various structures will provide immense help, and a therapist who is well trained in this field may become your best friend.

Other Issues

There are many other problems that can occur in a marriage, many of which are discussed below. If certain problems are not dealt with adequately, they can tear couples and families apart and lead to immense stress, quarrels, fighting, and even divorce. Again, before things escalate, seek assistance from professionals and others.

Job Loss

Losing a job can be another huge stressor for an individual and family. One of my friends was out of work for nearly two years. His wife wanted him to "take something, anything, to help pay the bills." Apparently, he wanted the *ideal* job. In the meantime, they racked up thousands of dollars in debt; and after three years of his working at a well–paying job, they were still paying it off. Sadly, it came between them and they have numerous issues to address.

In these circumstances, both people should be proactive, supportive, and understanding in solving problems. Unemployment funds are merely a stopgap and are not usually enough to replace a good job. Unfortunately, some people remain on unemployment assistance far longer than is necessary or even honest. On the other hand, finding a job can be exceedingly challenging and stressful. My heart goes out to those who struggle to find suitable employment to take care of themselves and their families.

Mental Illness

A mental illness diagnosis in a spouse can be disconcerting and challenging. Depression, Anxiety, Bi–Polar Disorder, Schizophrenia, Obsessive Compulsive Disorder, and Personality Disorders are a few of the possibilities. Any one of these can alter a family and a marriage in many ways—financially, socially, causing resentment, distancing, intensifying anger, needing to assume more responsibility, having to be like a single parent, and more. Medications can help, but if one chooses not to take medication or engage in counseling, the ramifications for the marriage can be dramatic. On the other hand, one who takes the initiative, takes prescribed drugs regularly, and works on their issues can be a wonderful partner. If a child is diagnosed, it can cause great stress to the parents and may sometimes affect the relationship.

Significant material has been written on mental illness, and treatments today are the best they have ever been. So if this is a situation in your family, please avail yourself of all the resources you can so you understand what to expect, how it may affect you, the use and possible misuse of medications, and how to access professional assistance. Remember that prescribed medications and over–the–counter drugs must be taken with a doctor's approval and advice, especially if a woman is pregnant or nursing. Counseling is one of the best resources.

Addictions

It is a well–known fact that substance abuse or other destructive addictions and a happy marriage usually cannot coexist. This is not something an abuser wants to hear. In fact, he or she is apt to be in gross denial about this fact, and it is a fact! A tremendous price is paid by the person's spouse and children. Feelings of abandonment, resentment, isolation, financial difficulties, violence, lack of intimacy, and sexual problems are just a few of the issues.

An addicted person also affects parents, family members, employers, coworkers, and friends, as well as causing a lasting impact upon their children. The damage done is not intentional, but it can create lifelong issues for the people disturbed along the way.

Denise was raised in a home where her parents fought continually. Her mother was harsh and often unreasonable, and her home life was conflicted and unpredictable. Low self–esteem became her nemesis. She grew to believe that all problems were her fault. Self–blame is typical for a child.

At about the age of 16, she came to realize that her mother was an alcoholic. Her father drank excessively on occasion and had a terrible temper even when he was not drinking. The damage to her life and that of her siblings was significant. While she and her sister were able to become healthy after leaving home through years of counseling, their brother turned out to be a heavy drinker and consumer of drugs. He engaged unsuccessfully in several treatment programs but eventually became quite ill and died at a young age.

When couples date, they may indulge in substance use or abuse together; but after marriage, especially if a family is wanted or a child is on the way, one of the partners may suddenly have a change of heart and want the twosome to grow up, be responsible, and prepare for having children. Hopefully, at least the mother recognizes the dangers to her child and ceases ingesting harmful substances. Intimacy, compassion, trust, and closeness can be destroyed, only to be replaced by anger, distrust, fear, resentment, and sexual dysfunction. Chronic use of alcohol or drugs in males frequently creates libido and impotence problems, while women may have menstruation issues, fertility complications, and a reduced desire for sex.

What was once a loving bond can become a shattered, unhappy, and miserable relationship. The partners may have a difficult time stopping the downward spiral, and the damage to children can be monumental. Help is always available when both parties are willing to seek it.

Other Addictions

Besides alcohol and street drugs, other addictions are harmful, as well. Sex, overeating, gambling, pornography, the internet, and excessive spending are a few examples. Pain medications and other prescription drugs are frequently overindulged in to the detriment of the family. Fetal Alcohol Syndrome is a horrible thing that some mothers who continue to drink pass on to the baby in utero. It can cause lifelong problems for a child.

Affairs

An affair can happen to anyone at any time. It is one of the primary reasons couples seek divorce. If people make a wise and loving choice in a partner, and their own values are such that they would not leave their spouse and children, they will do whatever it takes to repair any situation that gets in the way of happiness. Their commitment to their family and to the vows they made is stronger than any temptation they might encounter. They know better than to put themselves in tempting or vulnerable circumstances in the first place.

Unless someone is a serial cheater, unfaithfulness most often occurs in situations where couples are unhappy. The felt need for connection and understanding in such instances can be extremely compelling. And if sexual and emotional needs are not met, a partner is more susceptible to someone else, especially an exciting, sexy, attentive other person or one who is on the make.

If there is a hole in the asphalt of a road, what happens when it rains? Obviously, water fills up the hole. If there is discontent or disconnectedness in a relationship, a vulnerable partner can easily succumb to one who is willing to fill up the emptiness. Monogamy is a commitment, and it takes someone with firm marital loyalty and strong values to resist a persistent tempter or temptress.

If an affair occurs, a marriage can survive; however, both parties must be willing to work together to overcome the pain, hurt, and betrayal. Infidelity strikes at the very core of a marriage, and trust in the commitment and vows they made together is undermined. It can be devastating to both parties, but particularly to the person who has been betrayed. The hurt can be enormous, perplexing, and demeaning, and self–esteem can be severely compromised.

Typically, the betrayer wants the hurt feelings to be over with quickly. He or she has apologized and wants the other person to move on. However, even when forgiveness is offered, it can take a long time for the betrayed person to recover and trust again. Immense patience is required if healing and forgiveness are to ensue.

During their early forties, Bill and Jenny came in for counseling because Bill had had an affair. Jenny was preparing to file for divorce, but they decided to go to counseling. He had been unhappy for a while but had failed to communicate his concerns. He traveled frequently and would sit in airport bars looking quite sexy and available. There were plenty of women who hit on him. He succumbed more than once and even thought he was in love with one of the women.

It took some time, but gradually we worked through the couple's issues in counseling. They were able to express their deepest needs, make significant changes, and begin to rebuild their marriage. Bill changed his schedule so travel was minimized, and he no longer put himself in compromising positions. Jenny became more attentive and was able to meet many of his requests. Their love and commitment grew deeper than ever, and their precious children didn't have to suffer the turmoil of a divorce.

Pornography

Pornography is very common today, yet it can be almost as damaging to a relationship as an affair. A sample of over 4,000 individuals revealed that pornography harms the individual as well as the relationship. Since men are quite prone to respond to visual prompts, many are easily susceptible to an attractive woman, whether in person, in print, or on screen.

Ready access to the internet makes pornography available, affordable, and anonymous. A man who is into porn can do his best to hide his habit. But when his wife discovers it, she will most likely feel the same kinds of pain as if there had been an affair—shock, hurt, anger, and betrayal, as well as feeling useless and demeaned as a wife.

Frequently, a man doesn't understand her pain because he is viewing something on screen or paper. He may quip, "I'm not with some other woman, so what's the big deal?" Nevertheless, most women feel replaced, undesirable, and rejected. Her self–worth, self–image, trust, and safety are shattered. She starts to doubt even her most positive memories and experiences with her husband. In most cases, the marriage may not be over, but it will require some serious work and repair.

Kevin B. Skinner, PhD, a licensed marriage and family therapist, said: "Far too many couples don't know how to deal with pornography in their relationship. My research indicates that many women are experiencing trauma, and many men are struggling with compulsive behaviors and other mental health concerns like depression and anxiety. These real–life challenges make relationship bonding and connection much more difficult."

I've had several clients in this situation. The women are devastated and feel they are not enough, and the men then have a hard time responding to their partners. It definitely affects the close relationship they once had. Some get through it, and others do not.

More About Death

The death of a spouse, parent, or other significant person of course causes anguish and despair. Grief is a process. One does not recover, have closure, or have the grief simply go away, as so many people expect. It cannot be ignored, hurried, or bypassed. The diminishing of pain must and will only happen in its own time.

Sometimes, people avoid their emotions. This is a nonproductive coping strategy. Others overuse alcohol or other drugs, withdraw, or become overly involved to try to cover up their loss. As already stated, relationships may suffer, and divorces can occur. Much has been written on these topics, so use resources as necessary.

Medications can take the edge off the misery and allow a person to manage grief. Seeing a doctor, attending a grief group, or working with a counselor are valuable. Keep in mind that taking an antidepressant or anxiety medication is no different from taking a medication for high blood pressure, diabetes, or other condition. It's not a crime. When going through stress, the body's chemistry can be altered for a time. A medication can be of tremendous assistance and may only be needed temporarily.

Gender Roles

Until the 1960s and '70s, men generally were employed outside the home and women took care of the household and children. Women were commonly subservient to men and didn't work much outside the home. If they did, many were subjected to criticism.

Things began to change during those years when women wanted greater equality and shared responsibilities with their partners. In fact, the prevailing expectations for today are that if a woman works outside the home, the couple will divide household tasks equally. Though that may be their agreement, studies report that women still perform about 67% of home and child care and men take on 33%, including upkeep of cars, yard work, and maintenance matters.

One of the major grievances women express is that their husbands don't take enough responsibility. Those without a system for sharing tasks are more prone to tension and built–up resentments. So my advice is to develop a plan early on to solve problems before they occur. You can make a list of all the tasks, and then divide them up by who wants to do each one. Those that neither person wants to do can be drawn from a hat or just divvied up evenly, or the person who most wants the job done could take on that duty. Just make sure it all feels fair according to your mutual desires.

Fortunate is the woman who can stay at home, especially when her children are small. Or fortunate is the man who gets to be the stay–at–home dad, as discussed earlier. Yes, there are more homecare responsibilities, but that can be a nice thing.

Texting, Facebook, and Other Technology

Is technology destroying your social skills? Today, young people are constantly using social media, so much so that at times they barely speak to each other. I've even known of people who have broken off their relationship or engagement with a text message. How inconsiderate and cowardly is that? What happened to face–to–face communication, sharing real feelings, hearing the tone of voice, and seeing facial expressions? These provide so much more information and give parties an opportunity to discuss what is really going on.

A snail–mail letter or thank–you card is almost a thing of the past. One of my dear friends writes me letters every so often, and I treasure her efforts immensely. Writing emails and texts can be a quick and valuable means of communication in the right circumstances. They can also seem cold and unfeeling and sometimes are brimming with potential misinterpretations. Caution must be used these days with information shared on Facebook, Myspace, and Twitter, including photos, as those things might be used in negative ways by friends, non–friends, employers, and others.

For busy couples, texting each other during the day can be fun and nice. However, be careful about discussing sensitive issues. Misunderstandings are more apt to occur, and the situation might escalate unnecessarily. Wait until you can be calm and have time to have conversations in person, especially concerning controversial topics. Voice tone and facial expressions will clarify intentions and moods, whereas written words can be easily misinterpreted.

A Place for Anger

Anger is a normal and natural reaction to many of life's circumstances. It can even be a valuable behavior. For one thing, it helps us avoid harm. Remember the fight or flight response? It can also heal our hearts, teach us how to resolve conflict, and develop better functioning relationships.

In his book *The Healing Power of Anger: The Unexpected Path*, Dr. John Rifkin states: "I define anger as the natural healing energy that the body generates in response to an injury. This energy is meant to address or tend to the injury." He further says: "Understanding anger and getting past the stereotypes and misconceptions about anger can change your life and help you deal with every relationship more effectively."

We can grow and learn from our feelings and improve ourselves and our relationships when we use anger in productive ways. I highly recommend this book to dig deeper into anger. Its extensive and incisive information and notable case examples are definitely worth exploring.

The feelings of anger are very real and need not be suppressed; but the way in which they are handled can be productive or damaging. Anger can certainly be misused and abused. When angry behavior is ongoing, unrelenting, belittling, or hostile, it can become quite destructive. It is especially unhealthy for children to witness. If this kind of abuse is not controlled, it often turns physical, which is detrimental to all involved. Some expressions of anger can even be life–threatening. Please see Dealing with Anger, in Chapter IX.

Fighting, Quarreling, and the Desire to Be Right

There are many reasons why people fight—sex, money, what school the kids should go to, cleanliness, not enough time together, relatives, holidays, etc. But underneath it all is usually the desire to have one's own way. One or both partners want to be right. I have often asked the question, "Would you rather be right or have peace?" Most couples choose peace, yet they continue fighting. There are a few reasons for this.

Self–esteem might be the issue. If someone is wrong, they will feel bad or inadequate, and so they want their partner to agree on their rightness even if they are incorrect. Other people want power and control, all in an effort to maintain some sort of superiority.

I knew a wonderful man, actually my dear father, who wanted so badly to look good that he found some criticism for just about everyone. He was also brilliant, but he flaunted his expertise to others profusely. Near the end of his life, I discovered that his own insecurities were what caused him to wish to appear so knowledgeable and superior. I wish I had understood this at an earlier age. Perhaps it would have saved me some of my early insecurities.

Some people are habituated to fighting because it's what they saw growing up. They perpetuate the pattern, perhaps even unconsciously. Others hate that example so much that they have done everything in their power to be different from their families. Their desire for peace is very strong. However, I hasten to add that being passive and letting others be in control is not the answer. Everyone has a right to their own feelings and opinions. It's the way in which they are expressed that can be productive or non–productive. Often, just a few coaching or therapy sessions to learn new skills and communication tools will begin to solve the problem.

In other cases, the situation is more complex. Relationships can cause certain individuals to feel quite vulnerable and exposed if they reveal too much. Though it may sound strange, fighting can be an unconscious way of creating distance and feeling greater safety. This is a more serious problem and needs some deeper intervention in order to find resolution. Learning what is underneath such fears and helping people experience closeness without fear can create new pathways toward real intimacy.

The Twelve Biggest Causes of Marital Dissatisfaction

What follows are a few more irritating but usually reparable problems, provided that couples use good communication skills, make a sincere effort, and are committed to each other.

- **Finances**: All healthy marriages have disagreements over money, but it can cause serious and ongoing quarrels if not dealt with effectively. Discuss earning and spending money, staying within a budget, which bills to pay, saving, overspending, who will earn the money, and what to do when children come. A workable budget that is agreed to and followed is the most effective way to stay on course. Above all, communicate regularly about financial matters and approach your choices wisely.
- **Children and parenting**: Discuss and negotiate potential disagreements early on, well before they arise. How many children do you want, what rules and consequences, food, responsibilities, education, religion, etc.? While couples may have different patterns of parenting, it is to their benefit to be "joined at the hip." Kids learn quickly to play one against the other when they see they can manipulate or sway. It is also advisable to avoid making big decisions about the children without consulting one another.
- **Religion/spirituality:** Find agreement on how to raise your children. In order to do this, you will need to thoroughly explore and share your attitudes and preferences regarding religion or spirituality versus nothing. Hopefully, this was discussed before marriage. Do it at your earliest opportunity to avoid problems later.
- **Extended family and in-law issues**: Though family members may mean a lot to you, your marital relationship comes first. This can be a very touchy subject, but you must avoid letting others interfere. If people meddle, are too involved, or exhibit animosity, discuss possible solutions

together as a couple. Set boundaries you are both willing to keep. If families are not involved enough, find ways you can draw closer. Is an apology needed or can you take responsibility for your part in a challenging situation? Strive to heal any disagreement before a lot of time elapses or gets out of hand. And do your best to be joined together in how you want to handle each circumstance. No "Mother comes first." Your primary allegiance should be to your partner.

- **Sex/intimacy:** Discuss your sexual and intimate life: how often, when, where, satisfaction, monogamy, a wandering eye, infidelity, meeting each other's sexual needs, wanting too much, wanting too little. It's important to talk, no matter how difficult it may be, but always do it with respect.

- **Household responsibilities**: This can be a huge problem, so early on, discuss distribution of chores, who does what, and when. Breakdowns can happen if you let things go and the house becomes a shambles or if you are unwilling to help with the baby, chores, and family responsibilities. Again, you can work this out; but a gentle, unselfish, and loving approach is prudent for the best results.

- **Friendships**: Discuss your friendships with others, with whom, how often to get together, and what to do if you don't like the people whom your partner enjoys. Consider which people enhance or disturb your relationship. Make an effort to be with people who support and enrich your marriage. Discuss your wishes about socializing with and without each other.

- **Hidden expectations**: Are there things which one of you expects but you haven't discussed? The main solution here is to communicate. Discuss desires and expectations, then make agreements which you can each keep. Make lists and then live up to them.
- **Inability to communicate and solve problems**: Good communication is the key to a good relationship. Poor skills in talking, resolving conflict, or just sharing about yourself, your feelings, and your hopes and dreams can cause friction. Couples who do poorly in marriage don't know how to discontinue damaging arguments or how to avoid running away from issues. Review Chapter IX regarding communication tools.
- **Personality conflicts**: Differing personality and communication styles can cause many problems, such as being controlling vs. submissive, aggressive vs. passive–aggressive, extroverted vs. introverted, social vs. unsocial. These are only a few of the possibilities.
- **Annoying habits**: How someone chews food, bites their nails, frowns, irritating body language, infrequent bathing, smoking, etc. can be more than annoying. Be honest and share your feelings and desires with kindness and respect. Negotiate solutions.
- **Distractions:** Too much of any good thing can be destructive, such as too much TV, texting, computer games, talking on the phone, working all the time, spending too much time with extended family, etc. If these occur routinely, ask yourself or your partner why. What are you avoiding? Is it your partner? Is it communicating? Communication is the best healer. You just need to learn how to do it effectively.

The Four A's of Marital Unhappiness and Destruction

I strongly hope these issues don't involve you, but any or all can have a profound impact on your relationship if they occur. They are probably the most significant and destructive of all interpersonal problems—except for criminal activity, which is a totally different topic.

The Four A's:
> **Abuse** (emotional, verbal, physical, sexual)
> **Addictions** (drugs, alcohol, prescription drugs, gambling, etc.)
> **Adultery** (may be physical or emotional, depending on perception)
> **Anger** (severe, ongoing, irrational, or unrelenting)

As mentioned, many of the behaviors and issues you encounter can be repaired through a proactive approach: intense counseling, abstinence, hospitalization, AA programs, etc. I have counseled both individuals and couples through all of these conditions. Sometimes they were able to make changes and stay together, and sometimes not. It takes real desire, determination, and assistance to transform such difficulties and to weather the storm as a couple. Some of the "wrongdoers" do not want to change their habits, and so either a stalemate exists or the other partner must take a firm stand.

Most often, it is women who remain in an abusive marriage without recognizing the negative effects on themselves and their children. I believe that any of the four A's could be described as abusive. Some women are too frightened to leave or don't know how, where to go, or what to do. However, resources are plentiful if truly sought. Counseling, shelters, and family assistance are some of the options. If abuse is not dealt with in a meaningful and successful manner, an individual and family can be in actual danger. Sometimes divorce may be the most feasible option. If this is you, please seek help.

It is well known that children who grow up with these problems can develop major issues of their own that may take a lifetime to overcome. Some survive and become happy and successful people, but many others suffer serious damage requiring years of help later on.

Research has consistently shown that conflict between parents is the most consistent predictor of adjustment problems for children.
—Unknown

Remarriage

Divorce can happen, and unfortunately the death of a spouse may occur. If the remaining parent marries, some remarriages can be happy, effective, loving, and workable. Other times, they are unhappy and disharmonious, some of which may be due to the new partner being filled with jealousy or distrust, vying for time to be taken away from the children, not accepting the ex–spouse, envying the deceased spouse, or even disliking the children. This is a sad situation, especially for children.

The best advice I can give is to consider marriage *only* with someone who will accept you and your children with respect, dignity, and love and will treat your previous partner with respect and dignity. It is regrettable and even tragic when a new spouse interferes with a partner's relationship with his/her children. And it is certainly inappropriate to complicate the relationship with an ex–spouse out of jealousy, envy, spite, resentment, or any other reason.

And so, great care should be given in bringing a new person into the family until you are certain that he or she will fit into the existing dynamics in a way that works for everyone.

> *I may not be your first date, your first kiss, your first love, your first marriage. I just want to be your last everything.*
> —Unknown

Options for Action

- Seek professional guidance immediately if you have a special needs child.
- Locate grief counseling or therapy to help with grief, loss, or dealing with difficult situations.
- Of all the causes of marital unhappiness, note which ones are causing or may cause stress in your relationship. Discuss how you might solve them.
- Discuss finances frequently and create a budget together. If you disagree about spending money, get some help. This can cause lots of problems if not dealt with constructively.
- Talk about anger in your relationship—what it feels like and how to deal with it more effectively.
- Discuss any of the Twelve Biggest Causes of Marital Dissatisfaction and decide how to deal with any that are causing you problems.
- Identify behaviors that are most annoying or frustrating. Find ways to talk about them in a kind, non–accusatory way and discover solutions.
- Provide compassion and comfort when days and situations are tough.
- Practice sharing difficult problems using good communication skills.
- Find professional help if you cannot deal with the addiction or behaviors of your spouse.
- If there is abnormal behavior, depression, or mental illness, seek help immediately.
- Include one another in decision–making. Discuss which matters are acceptable for just one of you to decide and which decisions should be made jointly.

Chapter IX
Open, Honest, and Kind Communication Leads to Growth

Grant that we may not so much seek to be understood as to understand.
—Saint Francis of Assisi

What great advice from St. Francis! Certainly, understanding is required to create a happy relationship. Effective communication involves having the ability to share joys and sorrows, agree and disagree, and amicably handle whatever else is going on. It also means being willing to understand another's point of view, not necessarily being in agreement.

When you can be together without saying a word but feel one another's hearts, you speak reams. The best and most meaningful connections are made from the heart; and when you say things from your heart, you keep a relationship alive and vital. Some valuable skills will follow.

Effective Communication

Since words can be the source of understanding or misunderstanding, effective communication is one of the best skills you can ever acquire. Unfortunately, most of us didn't learn how to verbally communicate in our families, schools, or elsewhere.

Certainly, the adage "sticks and stones will break my bones, but words can never hurt me" is an absolute falsehood. Communicating negative or difficult messages without creating conflict or destroying trust is a tricky proposition but a skill worth developing. Words do hurt, so it is important to avoid saying anything disparaging or something that could be difficult for someone to forget.

Just being able to talk about everyday matters, feelings, joys, and sorrows is an indication of a good partnership. It is also imperative to learn to work through and resolve conflicts harmoniously by discussion, negotiation, and compromise.

Conflict is not a negative thing because at least you are communicating. Conflicts and disagreements are inevitable. However, speaking with intense anger, hostility, or "I'm right and you're wrong" can be very destructive. Some relationships can't survive such language, and it is especially harmful to children.

Elements of Communication

Research shows that the actual words spoken account for only 10% of our communication. Vocal tone—how the words are said—accounts for 40%. Body language and facial expressions account for 50%. How you implement all of these is central to the success of any relationship. The ability to manage stress in the moment and the capacity to recognize and understand your own emotions and those of the person with whom you are communicating are also aspects of effective communication.

As an aside, the above information helps clarify why written communication, emails, texting, etc. are often inadequate, and how misunderstandings, anger, and blame can transpire. If an argument emerges, make an agreement to preferably speak in person, or at least on the phone, so you can observe each other's cues and develop a greater ability to find resolution.

Learning good communication skills may seem rote at first, but the more you practice, the easier and more natural they will become. When you can speak together openly and respectfully, you can resolve conflict effectively. Then love and respect can flourish.

> *Communication is to a relationship what breath is to life.*
> —Virginia Satir

No Time to Talk

The revered therapist Virginia Satir is right. Communication is that important. Many clients tell me, "Oh, we don't have time to talk." Yes, children and work take a lot of time, but can't you fit one another into your schedule? Do you really need that cell phone on all the time? Is your work really so demanding that you don't have time for family? Are you spending a lot of time texting or emailing? How much time are you spending on web searches, social media, or video games? Do you have family dinners together, or is the TV on? Do you go to bed together?

"We have different schedules," or "I'm a night person," or "She goes to bed when the sun goes down" are all common refrains. So is "I have to be available all the time for work." Perhaps there is a better job in your future.

When *do* you have time for each other? What are you avoiding? Letting things build up because you don't make time to talk ends up consuming even more time when you finally do discuss a problem. In the meantime, you may be miserable, unhappy, and angry. If you haven't dealt with issues in a timely manner, try discussing them when they occur, or as soon as possible thereafter. If there is anger, take time out, and talk when you are both calm. And how about just sharing some pleasant moments, talking about—well, anything—peacefully?

> *Not having time for one another is a priority problem, not a time problem.*
> —Unknown

When you use your most effective communication skills to get to the bottom of disagreements, you will enhance your relationship. If you are not talking well together, think about switching things up. Make a schedule, if you must, to share important topics. With a little exploration, you *can* find time! You can always make room for what you think is important, right? The bottom line is that spending time together is important for your marriage because "Love is spelled TIME."

One client told me that her husband read that many couples only spend about 40 minutes talking over a week's time. That averages out to a mere 5.7 minutes per day. Pretty sad! So when they had attained their 40 minutes, one of them would teasingly say, "Well, I guess we don't have to talk any more this week." She said they talked much more than that, but they always got a good laugh, and the statistic was a good reminder to keep talking.

Communication with Your Children

Babies respond to music and loving talk even in the womb. They can also be negatively affected by arguments and hostility. From the time of birth, they learn to coo, smile, laugh, and make sounds by example. So how you talk with them and with each other teaches them how to behave. It is not uncommon for argumentative parents to cultivate unruly kids, obviously unintentionally.

And so it is never too early to establish a safe, nurturing, and happy environment as they grow. Love is spelled TIME for children, too. They need to experience precious moments together with family members, especially parents, in a secure atmosphere so they can grow, develop, and mature in a normal to extraordinary manner. Respectful communication between parent and child, as well as between parent and parent, helps them feel safe and secure.

Dillon's parents divorced when he was 10 years old. His father was sadly absent most of the time. His mother did the best she could, but she overindulged him to make up for her ex–husband's absence. She had to go to work every day and often left him unattended. Soon she married another man who was caustic and controlling. As the years went by, Dillon began mimicking his stepfather's language toward his mom. By age 15, he was out of control, and the stepfather didn't support his mother in any disciplinary actions. This family had a real crisis.

Nicole was also divorced with three children—two boys and one girl. She treated them with respect and communicated with them openly. She was interested in their lives, and they felt safe bringing any problems to her. She remarried, and her husband was also a valuable influence in their lives. They were joined together in how to raise the children, who developed beautifully. Even through the often tumultuous teen years, the kids remained respectful and obedient. Most of all, they felt safe and loved.

Yes, time together, along with respectful, open communication, will have a huge impact on a child's life. Never underestimate what happens under your own roof. You help create the paradigms of the future through your modeling.

A Few Ideas About Communicating

- First, find a good time to talk. You can ask, "Is this a good time to talk?"
- Be specific. Don't beat around the bush, but do it in a kind and gentle manner.
- Stay on target.
- It's okay to agree to disagree. Use talking to *understand* one another, not necessarily to agree.
- Address issues constructively and respectfully.
- Understand that disagreement and conflict are part of life and can be handled. Some people avoid conflict at all costs, but ignoring problems only creates more.
- Don't assume. Get clarification by asking unloaded questions stated clearly, concisely, directly, and kindly.
- Ask for a time out if things get heated.

Expressing Thoughts Tactfully

Sometimes couples have a difficult time sharing their feelings. Feelings that are not articulated in a desirable way may not go over well to one who is sensitive or feels vulnerable when critiqued, corrected, or told that something didn't work well. Even when done in a gentle manner, it can feel like overt disapproval. We are all vulnerable and apprehensive creatures at times. But in a marriage, events as well as communication need to function well for *both* people. If one partner stuffs feelings out of fear of recrimination for venturing into a delicate topic, resentments can fester and may end up creating distance instead of closeness.

This can be a very perplexing problem. So what is the answer? It certainly requires a diplomatic approach. Perhaps one or even both partners are wondering, "How can I express my thoughts so he/she won't take offense? I try and try, and no matter how I say it, I end up feeling awful."

One of the best ways I have found is to say to your spouse, "Honey, when I have something I want to tell you or discuss about our relationship, what is the best way I can say it? How can I tell you my thoughts in a way that will sound most caring and thoughtful to you?" Ask them to actually model the words they would like you to use.

Then what is required is a non–judgmental, listening ear, offering understanding and as much objectivity as possible. Make your partner feel safe with what has been stated, and digest the information so you can implement it. Perhaps then a discussion can emerge that takes both people's sensitivities into consideration. It means talking about talking, speaking in a way that will be well received.

Timing is also important. If either person is hungry, angry, tired, or stressed, it is not a productive time to bring up a controversial subject.

The reason this approach is usually successful is that it doesn't feel challenging or frightening. One spouse is truly interested in learning what is needed and wanted by the other in order to resolve differences, and it can be accomplished in a manner that will be appreciated rather than dreaded. The underlying attitude and the way thoughts are conveyed can make a mountain of difference in creating love and positive regard in the relationship.

Time Outs and Calming

What follows are some ways to make communication safe. Nothing can ever be resolved when people are upset. When anger or deep frustrations are present, a conversation is getting out of hand, someone is being irrational or unreasonable, your heart is racing, or one of you feels like throwing something, it is *way past* time to calm down. The signs of excessive distress need to be recognized.

Calling a time out could be the best solution. This means separating until you can be calm, reasonable, and rational. Nothing will be gained and a lot will be lost if you proceed when you are overly upset. Someone is likely to explode and resentments may build up. So ask for some space for a while.

It is critical that the other partner is willing and doesn't follow you around with a verbal cudgel. To calm yourself, go to a place where you can be quiet and undisturbed. Sit down, close your eyes, and take some deep breaths in and out. It helps to place your hand over your heart or belly as you slowly breathe. If it takes a few minutes or an hour to calm down, that's okay. Think about something positive—a beautiful scene, a happy moment, or a future event you would love to experience. You can also contemplate how you might approach the situation in a better manner.

Examine *your* part and what you can do or say to relax. Do this until you feel ready to talk. You can wait until later and resume talking after you are calm, but do not neglect to discuss whatever made one or both of you so upset. Either one can initiate the conversation, but it *must* be done. If you let things fester or stuff your feelings, they will just erupt at a time when you least expect them; so make it a habit to resolve things as quickly as possible.

Non–Verbal Communication

"Eyes are the window of the soul," it is said, because eyes convey our feelings, attitudes, and emotions. If you want to connect with a person, eye contact is necessary. Of course, if you are driving in a car, it is not possible; but when you can, provide attentiveness with your eyes. A fixed stare can be off–putting, but focusing varied attention on the face and eyes shows caring and interest in the other person.

An acquaintance of mine rarely looks at me when she talks. It is so unnerving; I just want to take her face in my hands and say, "If you want to talk to me, pleeeze look at me!" Eye contact is one of the first things I teach couples in joint sessions, as well as their body language. Do they appear open or closed, interested or uninterested, caring or not caring? One of my female clients tearfully said to her husband, "This is amazing. I've never seen you look at me like that ever since you proposed to me. Please don't stop!"

Have you ever considered how your body position seems to another person with whom you are communicating? If I as a therapist am looking away from my clients, not providing eye contact, and looking uninterested, how long do you think they will keep coming to me? It's the same with our spouse and children. How often does your wife come up and ask you a question or try to engage in conversation while you just keep texting your buddy? Or how often do you try to say something important to your wife, and she just keeps fixing dinner and fails to respond?

This happens every day in our communication with others. Observe other people and you will see yourself, whether good or bad. If you really want to be heard, then get the attention of the other person and say, "Honey, I want to ask you something. Could you take just a moment now?" Or ask, "When would be a good time for me to tell you about _____?"

Also, a seemingly innocent shrug or a sigh says a lot about how you feel, and so do facial expressions. Rolling the eyes or a slight movement of the lips speaks volumes. Our bodies reflect how we feel at any given moment. Disgust, fear, happiness, dominance, sympathy, and disinterest are just a few. So be aware of your body language.

The Speaker Skills

Use "I–messages," which focus on the problem, not the person, and are about stating *your viewpoint* rather than blaming or criticizing. Focus on good body language, eye contact, and neutral language. "I–messages" foster understanding and describe the feeling, the behavior that caused the feeling, and the impact the behavior has had on the speaker. "You–statements" sound accusatory and disrespectful.

> **I-_Statement_**: "I felt hurt and sad when you told Ted about my work problem, especially because I said it to you in confidence." You can follow up with a *request*: "What I'd like, honey, is for you not to talk about our personal problems with your buddies. Could you please do that for me?" The formula is "I feel _____ when you _____ because _____ . What I'd like is _____."

Versus

> **You-_Statements_**: "You always ____." "You never _____." "You are the most ____ ever." "I can't believe you _____." "I feel you are always _____." (The last two are *disguised* as "I–statements." Can you see that they are really "You–statements"?)

Listener Skills

> *Listening is a magnetic and strange thing, a creative force. The friends who listen to us are the ones we move toward, and we want to sit in their radius. When we are listened to, it creates us, makes us unfold and expand.*
> —Karl Menninger

Truly listening, really being there when someone is expressing himself or herself, can be a magical experience. Don't you feel wonderful when someone really hears and understands you? Unfortunately, many people think about what *they* want to say next instead of listening.

It's no wonder communication can get so distorted and misunderstood. The goals of effective listening are to build rapport, understand and empathize, convey clear messages, and break down barriers.

The skills are:

- Be aware of your body language—posture, facial expressions, and eye contact— which show genuine interest. Appearing upset or disinterested will be an immediate turn–off to decent communication.
- Use an amicable tone.
- Reflect/mirror what you heard. "I think I heard you say_____." "What I understood was_____."
- Ask clarifying or other questions. "Did you mean_____?" "Did I understand that _____?" Or "What can I do to_____?"

Challenge yourself to remain neutral and calm without an agenda and without analyzing or making interpretive or defensive comments. Letting things build up never works, so handle issues in the moment or as soon thereafter as feasible. And do so respectfully, reflecting back what you heard. Continuing to talk or asking questions doesn't necessarily mean you agree. You can *agree to disagree* when agreement isn't possible. Your purpose should be to *understand* what the other person is conveying; that is very powerful! When in doubt, ask questions. Always be aware that you might be projecting or making up stories. Check it out by asking.

Why People Don't Listen or Acknowledge Others

There are a few reasons for this:

- They don't choose to.
- They don't care.
- They disagree with you and are unwilling to talk about it.
- Their needs are not being met, so they dig in.
- They have a need to be or feel in control.
- They don't want to be challenged or changed.
- They are afraid to or don't have confidence.

Don't let this be you. I hear so many complaints about one partner not listening or not seeming to care. It is one of the major reasons for stress in a relationship. Think about it: Friendships don't continue very long if people don't share, listen, and acknowledge one another. Marriage is no different and is an even more important reason to listen.

If someone won't talk, just persist nicely and let them know why it is important to you. Maybe they will and maybe they won't, but at least you've tried. In any case, things will work out much better if you utilize the skills we are discussing.

Safety

I always discuss the issue of safety with my clients. If a person doesn't feel safe, he may fear he will be attacked and will shut down. So consider that if honesty and real sharing aren't occurring, it is likely the other person *doesn't feel safe* communicating. Keep this in mind with children, too. A person will only feel safe if they are listened to, heard, and not criticized or judged.

If she admits, "I ran out of gas today," he might angrily respond with, "I told you it was getting low. Why in the heck don't you just keep it filled up? It's not my fault." Imagine how different it would be if he replied, "Oh, that's too bad, Sweetie. I'm glad you're home. So what did you do?" If someone is always afraid they will be chastised, they will shut down.

> *Jill constantly complained to her friends about her husband. "Roger never shares his feelings, and he never tells me what's going on at work. He avoids talking to me, and I just can't stand his attitude." After hearing her repeatedly gripe and complain about her husband, Martha finally got brave enough to say, "Do you talk to Roger and criticize him like you do when you talk to me? If so, I'm not surprised he won't talk to you. You sound so caustic. Is it possible he fears he will be attacked?"*

> *Jill was pretty angry at Martha for a while, but it caused her think about how she treated her husband. When she finally admitted that she was often critical of him and others, she changed her approach. After a period of time, he began to feel safe sharing with her, and their relationship improved greatly. Eventually she even apologized to Martha.*

The Spectrum of Communication

There are many choices in the ways people communicate. One can be deeply interested in someone and speak to them in an introspective and sharing manner, or they can simply converse about functional or logistical matters. Sometimes, the latter is how people talk to a spouse or child.

I don't recall where I found the list below, but it has been very useful. Look at the categories and see how you and your spouse speak most of the time. If you usually use the top three, consider how you could expand your range by discussing more meaningful topics.

- **Greeting:** Saying hello, how are you? Giving a nod, wave, or simple gesture.
- **Superficial or casual:** Asking how are you doing, how did work go, etc. It involves scheduling, routine, insignificant, or even meaningless interactions.
- **Functional or logistical:** Sharing information and observations. Working out details, some problem–solving. Expressing some feelings, opinions, or venting, but without an effort to understand.
- **Intellectual or philosophical:** Sharing concepts, thoughts, opinions, ideas. Engaging in discussions, deliberation, debates.
- **Introspective sharing:** Exhibiting sharing, bonding, and connecting. Talking about feelings and having a desire to understand. There is an ability to resolve issues and to explore expectations, desires, values, and goals. Close feelings, intimacy, and love are expressed.
- **Unspoken or intuitive:** There is a deep connection with meaningful sharing of feelings and viewpoints. There is an ability and desire to anticipate the needs and wants of others. Caring and closeness exist. In a loving relationship, there is heartfelt intimacy and shared love. Sometimes people are able to communicate without words, sensing what the other is thinking or feeling.

How is *your* communication? Where do you fall on the above spectrum with your partner, children, and others? Do you share with a desire to understand, or do you just talk about superficial or logistical things? Those in exceptional relationships share thoughts, ideas, heartfelt feelings, and goals, as well as loving words and actions. Of course, casual and logistical topics are necessary, but in your marriage, make a concerted effort to implement the ideas in numbers four, five, and six above, and you will have attained a higher level of relating.

Barriers to Verbal Communication

Everyone uses some of the following approaches from time to time, often without thinking. They are truly barriers and will shut down communication and cause an adult or child to feel unsafe faster than just about anything else. Which of these do you do at times?

- Moralizing
- Dominating
- Judging
- Criticizing
- Blaming
- Demanding
- Anger
- Yelling
- Interrogating
- Interrupting
- Controlling
- Distracting
- Placating
- Labeling

- Mini–lecturing
- Sarcasm
- Using belittling humor
- Making fun
- Sermonizing
- Rudeness
- Offering solutions without being asked
- Giving suggestions without being asked
- Sympathizing instead of empathizing
- Having a superior, know–it–all attitude

Do you like any of these to be used on you? I certainly don't. So be aware of your patterns and work on changing any that are ineffective.

The Blame Game

If understanding and acceptance of differences are lacking, couples tend to blame one other and wait for their spouse to meet their needs before they meet their spouse's needs.

This = IMPASSE.

Ingrid had grown up in a family where she was made the cause of anything negative that went on. As a child, she was always getting in trouble, even when she thought she was being obedient. Over time, she developed a way of being defensive and putting the onus on others so she wouldn't look bad. In her marriage to Ralph, she frequently attacked him with put–downs, blame, and sarcasm.

When he had almost had enough, they came for therapy. Ralph discovered that he was part of the problem in that when she attacked him, he became defensive and blamed her for everything. She also saw that her criticisms were pushing him away. Within a few sessions, they were able to change their dysfunctional "blame game" pattern. They learned more about one another's past experiences and began to take individual responsibility for their part in disagreements. As a result, they developed a more considerate attitude toward one another.

This dynamic is repeated over and over in families, schools, governments, and countries. Blame is rampant, people are unwilling to take ownership, problems persist, and battles erupt. No wonder there is so much conflict in the world. In marriage, blaming the other person is particularly destructive. It creates distance and destroys intimacy. Who wants to be loving or romantic in such an atmosphere?

Sometimes, blaming others is simply a habit learned from families, as was the case with Ingrid. Regardless of how ineffective it was, she learned to use blame as a coping strategy in order to look good. Continuous blamers may be afraid that they will look bad if they are not right, and so to preserve their own self–image, they resort to blaming others and refuse to take responsibility for their own contributions.

And so it is prudent to be responsible for your part of any situation rather than blaming someone else. You can apologize, which will help get you back into harmony. You will be healthier and happier because, as we know, stress can create health and other problems.

Shut Down or ShOut

Start your communication when you and the person with whom you are speaking are not **SHUT**—**S**tressed, **H**ungry, **U**pset, or **T**ired. If you do, one of you may **SHUT down** or **SH(O)UT out.** Think of "O" as being **O**verwhelmed, which could lead to shOuting. So avoid serious conversations if any of these are present. Timing is essential because nothing can be resolved when you are upset and angry. It's like trying to reason with a drunk.

It's best to talk about sensitive subjects when there is no stress, so learn the signs well. Your body will let you know. Remember the *Time Out* strategy so you can calm down before trying to resolve an issue. Also, humor is a great stress reliever.

In your marriage, be willing to compromise. That way, both win something and lose something, but it feels fair. You might also agree that sometimes he gets his choice and another time she gets her choice. Negotiate differences with openness, honesty, and kindness using good communication skills.

Dealing with Anger

Anger is a very real, acceptable, and appropriate emotion. How you *express or handle anger* is the issue. Taking out anger on yourself or others can be costly in many ways and can be especially damaging to children. An angry person often does not act in proportion to the importance or significance of the situation and may react in hostile or destructive ways. When you learn to express anger appropriately, you can begin to heal. It will also greatly reduce potential conflict with your spouse and others. Everybody wins.

My model of anger is to look at it in layers:

Anger is real. It can be expressed along a spectrum: outwardly, inwardly, or somewhere in between.	***ANGER***
Underneath anger is hurt, pain, fear, rejection, invalidation, or another *strong emotion*.	***PAIN HURT FEAR***
Underneath the strong emotion is an unmet *need*, such as feeling valued, secure, supported, seen, acknowledged.	***UNMET NEED***
Underneath that is a *communication problem* on either side—unexpressed, conveyed harshly, ignored, discounted, unheard, or misunderstood.	***COMMUNICATION***

When the layers of our own anger are understood, it is much easier to develop effective ways of handling and expressing it in a way that is not damaging to ourselves or others. And when the layers of another's anger are understood, it is easier to deal with it more effectively and handle the current stressor.

It is valuable to allow yourself to feel your feelings. However, you always have a *choice* about how you *express* anger or any other strong emotion. You may choose to either *act* or *react*. Though you feel things deeply, you can control your behavior and the manner in which you communicate. Think of a time when you were angry. Was it outwardly expressed or inwardly felt? What was the strong feeling underneath? What was your unmet need or needs? Was your upset communicated or received?

Unresolved Conflict

To me, the biggest problem in relationships is when people are unable or unwilling to resolve conflict. Obviously, conflicts can discharge in friendships, romantic relationships, families, and workplace settings. Variances exist in the willingness of people to find solutions. The matter will either come to resolution or be left unresolved, sometimes for decades, and sometimes even for a lifetime.

Those who can agree to disagree have usually been able to talk; at least they understand one another's thoughts. They recognize there will never be agreement, so they let go and allow matters to be what they are. They find compromise, allow independence, or simply realize that they will never see eye to eye. This approach takes mature and responsible individuals who desire to maintain harmony.

It becomes quite serious when an issue erupts and one or both parties don't want to discuss the matter. They keep things inside to fester or possibly escalate. The other party may attempt to explain or resolve the concern; but it goes nowhere because of defensiveness, not wanting to be vulnerable, worry they won't be heard or understood anyway, or a fear of reprisal. They may avoid, stonewall, withdraw, throw out sarcasm, or engage in perpetual arguments.

It's always best to make your best efforts to resolve the conflict. Other possibilities are to let go, accept the differences, or set healthy boundaries. Sometimes, things are said at stressful moments or without thinking, and so apologies are always advisable so the situation doesn't worsen.

In marriage, it is critical to endeavor to work things out. If people develop skills and tools to provide *safety* for one another, relationships can be repaired and move forward. If not, resentments, anger, hurt, or disrespect can persist for years and years. I have seen this far too often in my practice and in relationships in my environment. I urge you to look at Chapter X for other tools that can help keep your relationship strong if you utilize them.

Ten Guidelines for Handling Conflict

Here are a few guidelines you could agree to abide by when a disagreement occurs:

- Use a *Time Out* if the situation begins to escalate. Make an agreement in advance that either of you can ask for a time out. If that isn't possible, find a hand signal you both understand. The other must agree not to pursue and to allow the needed space. The person who called the time out should then arrange an opportunity to finish the discussion when things are calm. This technique should not be used to avoid talking. It isn't necessarily easy for the one who needs to get things resolved now, but it is essential when things are getting out of hand.

- No yelling or cursing. Keep your emotions calm and respectful.
- Acknowledge feelings and viewpoints before working on or presenting solutions. It is best to talk/acknowledge *feelings* before *facts* before trying to resolve the matter.
- Examine your intention. Is your goal to be right, making the other person wrong, or to preserve the relationship and foster love? Find a way to do the latter.
- Seek to discover the facts. What are your common goals, and what do you need from one another in order to find resolution? It isn't necessary to assert who is right.
- Stay with the issue and don't air everything in the laundry basket. Be specific and use examples so the situation can be better understood.
- Be open to the fact that you may have made a mistake or may have been the cause of the conflict. Your style of interacting may have led to the dispute. Apologize as needed and take responsibility for your part.
- Be willing to listen to the other person and seek to understand. You don't have to agree, but you do need to respect each other's viewpoints.
- Discuss issues as soon as possible so they don't escalate. You might schedule a time once a week to talk about your relationship. Share joys, positive aspects, and problems, and work through issues.
- Reserve time for dating, having fun, and going out together. Don't forget to plan for or create occasions for physical intimacy, as well. Spontaneity is always special.

Conflict Can Be Messy

Lots of skills and theories about conflict have been expressed above. Though it is not an easy topic, I am sure that if you implement the materials you have read, you will be able to approach disagreements more effectively. Clearly, we can't get through this life without conflict. It is completely normal and no one is immune. Opening up a conversation about a conflict without being angry, mean, or sarcastic can be quite perplexing—that is, if one even thinks about how to proceed. Much of the time, people just dive in with accusations and blame in a vitriolic or caustic manner.

Obviously, when individuals don't see eye to eye and one or the other has a set position, disagreements can erupt quickly and even escalate to an injurious pitch. Conflict is never tidy, but many things in life are not tidy. Cleaning house, repairing a car, and building a deck all cause disruption that will be remedied only after the job is complete and the mess is cleaned up.

Take the example of cleaning out your bedroom closet. It's a really messy job. Clothes and shoes lie all over the floor, on the bed, on the dresser. You may find disgusting things in there, such as a lost bottle of sour baby's milk, dust bunnies that would send the rabbits running, and hordes of other unwanted items. Garbage bags are lying around, and the clutter is almost revolting. But to achieve order, you must get things out of the closet where you can see what needs to be done. Only then can you get rid of what is unnecessary and put it back in an orderly fashion.

It's the same way in resolving a relationship dispute. It can also be a messy job. But, as stated many times, nothing can be resolved while anger or resentment are present. So here's a roadmap:

- Let the dust settle. Take a time out until you can be calm.
- Think of the issue you want to discuss. Write down your thoughts, if that would prove helpful.
- Come together and do your best to use good communication skills.
- It may be uncomfortable (and even messy), but listen to each other and get out your viewpoints so you know where each person is coming from. Attempt to appreciate their thoughts and feelings. It doesn't mean you agree. It just means you hear and grasp what they are saying.
- It really helps to acknowledge the feelings each person has before trying to look at solutions.
- If tensions still run high, as they might, stop again, take some deep breaths, and continue only when calmness reigns.
- Then you can seek a solution. If it's not a win/win for both of you, then find something that is at least workable. Compromise can be a powerful tool if used properly. Perhaps it will balance out in the long run.

Sometimes you have to be direct, but you can do it with charity, with generosity. Your viewpoint is important, but so is your partner's. That means laying things out and seeing what needs to be done—what you can discard (anger, hostility) and what you can throw away (perhaps a "my way or the highway" attitude). When you do that, you can usually find a workable solution.

Projection

Projection is a psychological term meaning that someone projects or imagines that something is true when it may not be true. It's a defense mechanism in which people make up stories and "project them onto a screen" as truth. One ascribes one's own thoughts, motivations, desires, and feelings to another or makes assumptions.

For example, if an individual criticizes someone of color, even for a legitimate reason, some would claim that person is a racist, which may be entirely false.

Another example is that a wife talks a lot about her male colleague at work and her husband makes up a story that they have romantic feelings for one another. He may even project/make up that they are having an affair and begin making accusations. She is completely innocent of his charges and can't comprehend his attitude. You can imagine the source of tension and anger that can produce.

Here's another marital example: A spouse comes home from work. He is grumpy and out of sorts. She thinks/makes up/assumes it's about an earlier interaction between the two of them. She gets grouchy herself and treats him poorly because she inaccurately thinks he is blaming her for something. Pretty soon the two are snapping at each other, and the evening becomes a wreck.

In reality, he had an issue with his boss but brought his upset home. His wife could have said, "Honey, you seem upset. What's going on?" or "Is it something about us?" This would have given him a chance to tell her what happened. Of course, it would have been even better if he had initially told her he was upset because of a work issue and not with her or the family. So you can see, it is possible to get at the truth without an argument. What a more peaceful world it would be if we could all think ahead to this degree; but we are not usually so forthcoming.

Everyone makes up stories from time to time, but if you become aware that you might be doing it, you can save lots of heartache. So what is the answer? This topic could be discussed in great depth because it is so universal; the short answer, though, is that you need to deal with your unconscious feelings. Ask questions, talk about it, think internally, and use common sense. Above all, don't assume the worst until you find out what is actually true. Most disagreements and relational problems are a result of projecting, so be a person who is reasonable and rational.

Assertiveness

I have talked a lot about being kind, gentle, calm, negotiating, compromising, and other affirmative behaviors. However, I do not want this to be mistaken for weakness, defenselessness, or powerlessness. Quite the contrary. Assertiveness is a way of being in which people stand up for themselves. They are not aggressive, passive, or passive–aggressive, but they maintain respect for both themselves and others. You will see the differences in the descriptions below of the Four Communication Styles.

While one may not always feel confident and self–assured, they can practice interfacing with the world in that way. For a passive person, being assertive can feel like aggression. It is not, but it may need to be learned and practiced in order for the passive individual to feel comfortable. Assertiveness feels self–embracing and empowering. Speaking can be done in a diplomatic and inclusive way so others feel respected.

One way to be assertive is to learn to say no when something isn't right for you. You can also express your needs and feelings clearly, let go of guilt and fear, avoid wanting to be right or perfect, and communicate in a clear and direct way. Most people prefer that others use assertiveness to communicate with them.

Four Styles of Communication

Note the styles you most identify in yourself, your partner, and others. Decide which one you prefer, and make attempts to alter your type if you dislike the one/ones you exemplify.

> **Aggressive**—I Win/You Lose: Seeks personal power or gain through taking advantage of others. The manner is insisting, dominating, pushy, overbearing, hostile, superior, thoughtless, threatening, and bossy.

> **Passive–Aggressive**—I Lose/You Lose: Aims to manipulate others to gain advantage. It is indirect and covert by hiding intentions and misleading others. A person may stuff feelings but dig in by being resentful, grudge–carrying, dishonest, bitter, revengeful, two–faced, phony, confusing, sarcastic, and/or using double messages. The person gives compliments but badmouths others at the same time. They think they win, but they don't.

> **Passive**—I Lose/You Win: Allows others to invade, control, or take advantage of you. This style defers to others, is apologetic, acquiescing, retreating, timid, inhibited, unexpressive, insecure, and self–denying. It also invites domination and aggression.

Assertive—I Win/You Win: Expresses thoughts, feelings, beliefs, and preferences honestly and openly. Communication is clear, direct, aware, honest, flexible, confident, open, negotiating, responsible, and considerate of others.

Honesty

If you tell the truth, it becomes the past. If you tell a lie, it becomes an uncomfortable part of your future.
—Unknown

Integrity and honesty are absolutely essential to a good relationship. They are the only ways to truly understand one another and promote love. They also create safety and security. In addition, trust is created, which is absolutely essential for happiness. Honesty can be painful, especially if there is something uncomfortable to share; but it is vital if a loving, strong bond is to be formed. A single lie discovered is enough to create doubt about every truth stated, and it can take a long time to rebuild trust.

Being open with thoughts and feelings is also part of honesty. I sadly recall a relationship I was in. The other person stuffed his feelings and would not or could not discuss any issues—positive or negative. Since I am a communicator, I wanted to talk about our lives, discomforts I was feeling, or conflicts we were experiencing. Perhaps then I didn't do it in the best way possible, but I believe I was kind and open for a long period.

However, as time went on, I learned it was best to stuff my feelings. Resentments built up, and I'm sure my communication conveyed my frustrations. I even got sarcastic at times. He didn't complain about that either. Truly, I didn't like the way we were being with one another at all, and I didn't enjoy how I felt inside or behaved outwardly. As much as I wanted to, I didn't even feel safe sharing my joys and happiness.

Do not do what I did. Do your best to be open about challenging issues. If you don't, they will increase over time and affect the relationship in adverse ways. The tools in this chapter will help a lot if you use them.

Has your wife ever put you on the spot and asked, "Honey, do I look fat in this dress?" What would happen if you said, "Yeah, those stripes really accentuate your stomach." You just might be put outside in the doghouse with Rufus. But what if you said, "I love the way you look in your blue dress. Why don't you wear that?" Yes, sometimes it's best to be sensitive and tactful rather than brutally honest.

Dishonesty

Most people have a need to know their partner's feelings, thoughts, joys, sorrows, likes and dislikes, past events, future goals, and so much more. If you only care about yourself and are not invested in the relationship, then you may become deceitful or shut down, both of which can cripple your marriage to the point of no return.

Dishonesty is the biggest destroyer of love, and trust will be greatly diminished. Romantic affairs are the worst. It is upsetting when information that partners should share is hidden.

One woman I knew was devastated when she found out her husband had had a brief marriage several years before. He didn't think it was important to tell her, but she thought it was very important. Another friend's husband waited six years, until after all their children were born, to tell her he was gay. It was devastating, and the betrayal was enormous. These massive lies caused destruction in both marriages. Both major and minor topics should be brought into the open as early as possible.

A strong motivator for lying is an effort to protect oneself. A child will lie about taking three cookies instead of one. Why? So he won't get in trouble. A teen may lie that the reason she is late is because the car ran out of gas. Why? So she won't get in trouble. A wife may lie that she didn't hit the telephone pole and that another car hit her. Why? So she won't get in trouble. Hmm. Again, if there is open, honest, and respectful communication instead of deception, safety is created and the truth can be said without fear of reprisal—that is, if the partner is kind and a bit of luck is present. There may be consequences, but they can be handled kindly.

Share Your Feelings

Now that you have some tools, find occasions to talk. Once a week, sit on the bed, look at one another, and hold hands. How upset can you be doing this? If you start by discussing things that are going well, the negatives won't seem so threatening. Just be calm, considerate, and assertive.

> Sit calmly in a comfortable position on the bed or couch. Then hold hands and share back and forth one thought at a time for several passes: *"I appreciate you because _____."*

Do the same thing with *"I feel close to you when
_____."* Then switch to *"I feel distant from you
when _____."* Don't discuss; just share your
sentences briefly with no responses.

In the same fashion, share *"Something I love about
our relationship is _____,"* and *"Something I'd like
to be different is _____."* Even though you may be
mentioning potentially stressful topics, you can do
so in a neutral and loving way. This helps create
safety. It's easy to let things escalate, so keep your
voices calm and respectful, and maintain a caring
body posture.

When you feel comfortable doing this exercise,
you can each take five minutes and say anything
you want, then let your partner do the same.
Again, the key is to be kind and courteous in your
expressions, or this will not work. Later, you can
do it for 10 minutes.

Get to Know One Another

Do you know what her favorite ice cream is, her
favorite color, where she would most like to travel, how
she would like your lives to be five years from now? Do
you know what car he would most like to have, his favorite
dessert, how he thinks having a baby has changed your
relationship, his unfulfilled dreams? If not, these are only a
few of the fun discussions you can have. Such questions
can be enjoyable to do with children, too, when they are
old enough.

Ask open–ended questions, such as, "Tell me about
how you handled the situation with Harry today," instead

of a closed–ended question like, "Did you and Harry work things out?" Do you see the difference? One question invites conversation; the other invites a simple yes or no answer. If you think your partner isn't very talkative, examine how you encourage or don't encourage conversation. Be specific and really care about knowing one another. Do this with children, too, and you will enjoy much more interaction.

A Soft Style

When my husband and I were talking about this topic, he said, "Don't underestimate the power of womanhood. A woman who approaches things in a tender, caring way can melt a man's heart." The same is true in the way a man approaches a woman. Defensiveness, harshness, criticism, or anger will not make things better. They will only create more defensiveness, harshness, and anger.

It's difficult to come back from a harsh approach, though it can be done. Just say you are sorry and that you want to find a better way to talk things out. Take responsibility for your words and actions. Believe me, your spouse (and children) will be much more willing to listen.

The Truth Sandwich

When you decide to talk about a challenging topic, *create safety* for the other person. How do you do that? Begin by talking about yourself and your feelings using "I–statements."

For example, use the Truth Sandwich. Imagine a hamburger. Use the top bun to say something positive. Then, instead of "but" (because people get their guard up and may shut down when you say "but"), say, "at the same time" or "I've been thinking...," etc. Then say the meat of your subject—what you don't like—in a kind way, using those I–messages. Follow this up with the bottom bun, with something like, "I'm saying this because..." (I care, I want us to be closer, etc.) Then make your suggestion, request, or create an opening to talk.

> *Example:*
>
> "Honey, I appreciate that you've been working so hard at your job and that things have been stressful for you." (Bun)
>
> "At the same time,..." (Lettuce)
>
> "I've been feeling sort of down recently, and I wanted to let you know. I think it may be because we've been doing our own thing and not spending much time together." (Meat)
>
> "I love and miss you and wonder if we can talk about it. I'd like to come up with some solutions so that we can be together more." (Bun)

You sandwich your complaint/frustration between two nice statements and include a request at the end which is a non–threatening, inclusive, truthful, and gentle approach. This is much more effective than saying, "Why are you always at work? You don't get home until late and I'm sick and tired of being alone and having you ignore me. I don't like being a doormat one bit!"

Stop Complaints and Nagging

"For heaven's sake, Richard, that's not how you iron a shirt. You start with the collar." "Why did you warm the bottle like that?" "Why didn't you stop Sammy from riding his bike on the grass?" "I've asked you a dozen times to clean out the garage." Blah, blah, blah!

Poor Richard! He feels he can do nothing right and soon stops doing anything because he is always made out to be wrong. Then she complains that he doesn't help. Can you blame him? She sounds like a grouchy, depressed wife, or even like a nagging mother. What guy wants to be married to his mother, anyway? Richard wants a loving wife. Give the man some space! How important is it for a shirt to be ironed a certain way? Everyone needs praise, validation, and generous thanks. They don't need criticism, sarcasm, or anger. So pick your battles.

I'm not saying to stuff your feelings, but do use good communication and be kind, whether speaking your truth or receiving data. Have a gentle approach and use the information gathered to improve your relationship, not to beat up yourself or one another.

In your discussions about communication, it would be easy for each partner to claim that the other is wrong or use blame when some of the skills are not used properly. You can avoid doing this by practicing using the skills until they are second nature. It may take some gentle persistence, but you *can* develop new patterns together.

Communication skills are essential to share and convey our ideas and knowledge. They are the foundation for our success. If your skills are lacking, begin first by focusing on your listening skills. Strengthen these, and you'll be in a very solid position.
—Dr. Anil Kr Sinha

Options for Action

- Discuss how much you talk together. If it is not much, talk about how to create more time to talk. Since safety is the key, what makes you feel safe in bringing up and discussing topics? What makes you feel unsafe?
- Practice using the Speaker and Listener skills until you feel comfortable using them.
- Identify the barriers to communication you may be using and which ones your spouse is using. Determine to eliminate those and replace them with effective communication.
- Determine your level in the Spectrum of Communication. Note how you can improve.
- Do the Four Communication Styles exercise and identify your primary style. Practice being Assertive, if that is not your main style.
- Talk about the best ways to resolve conflict. Which ones in the list above do you have difficulty implementing?
- Assess how well you know one another. Ask each other questions, like, "What is your favorite color, car, movie star, movie, etc.? How do you feel about _____ candidate or the issue _____?"
- Discuss the actions that make you feel most loved.
- Just be together and talk about your joys and dreams.
- Spend 30 minutes often just talking about your lives without TV or computers to distract.

Chapter X
Strategies, Solutions, and Exercises for Enhancing Your Marriage While Parenting

Too often we underestimate the power of a touch, a smile, a kind word, a listening ear, an honest compliment, or the smallest act of caring, all of which have the potential to turn a life around.
—Leo Buscaglia

It's time for solid strategies, solutions, and exercises for enhancing or perhaps reigniting the spark in your marriage, even in the midst of changing diapers or picking your child up from soccer practice. At any stage, I hope you recognize the value of working on your relationship while enjoying one another. You can love someone with all your heart, but unless you bring your best self to the forefront, your relationship will stagnate. Even the happiest marriages require dedication, commitment, wise decision-making, and thoughtful, deliberate actions. And don't forget ROMANCE!

There are no Options for Action to consider in this chapter because I recommend that you practice the skills and do the exercises as they are listed. This requires some planning and scheduling, because a lot of these you'll want to do without worrying about the kids. Even if your marriage is doing well, I am confident you will benefit from them.

Contemplation Skill

Several of the exercises will suggest that you contemplate, imagine, or envision something. To do this, sit in a quiet, undisturbed space when you are feeling relaxed and stress–free. Close your eyes and take a few slow, deep breaths. Let your mind relax and contemplate what you are considering. When you feel finished, open your eyes. Write down your thoughts and/or discuss them with your partner. Use good communication skills to assist you in discussing matters calmly and respectfully

Create Your Vision

Create a vision for your marriage and your family. Use the Contemplation Skill and consider what you personally want to represent to your family and to the world. Then imagine how you want life to be as a couple and as a family. What are your goals and dreams? Discuss your thoughts together and imagine yourselves and your family down the road. What will you be doing, feeling, and saying, and how do you want your family to be? Do this without judgment.

Exercise: Record your thoughts describing your personal vision, then compare your lists and create a joint list. A few examples are:

- We are affectionate with each other.
- We love intimacy—emotional and sexual.
- We settle our differences peacefully.
- We are financially secure.
- We are in agreement about training our children.
- We have date nights on a regular basis.

- We can talk easily together, sharing our joys, concerns, and desires.
- We enjoy each other and have fun together.

Values

Values are the fundamental elements that have great meaning to you. They are guiding principles, those matters that are vital to your life. Knowing and living true to them gives you power to make choices, find greater fulfillment, and have the life you truly desire—both individually and as a couple. If you have a value but are doing other things which do not honor what you value, then you might want to look at how you are leading your life.

For example, if you revere spending quality time together but you work so much that you don't have time to talk and share, then spending time together must become a higher priority than working. Your actions need to support what is most important to you. And whatever you do, remember that is what you are modeling to your kids.

Phil was a workaholic. He left for work at 6:30 a.m. and rarely got home before 7:30 p.m. He hardly saw the children and was always too exhausted to help Joan. When she attempted to talk about it, he would say, "I'm just trying to make a good living for my family. What do you expect?" She told him she just wanted him and didn't care about a bigger house, a boat, or a newer car. She just wanted her husband, her companion, and her lover. She also noted that the children were unable to spend much time with him.

Phil valued his family, but his actions weren't compatible with that. Though earning a living was important, he had to look at what he valued more—things or family. If his wife had constantly complained about the house being too small or that they didn't have enough money to furnish it tastefully—and she said she wanted him home more—they would have had a real conflict.

Exercise: First make separate lists of your personal values, and then come together to create a joint list. Discuss each item and only write it down if you both agree. If something is similar but not exactly the same, just change the wording to reflect the desires of each of you combined into one concept. Your lists will help you avoid anything that goes against your values; instead, your values will help to guide your steps.

> *Examples: I/we value: Closeness, quality time together, our children, good music, loving acceptance, monogamy, harmony, compassion, service to others, our religious path, teamwork, integrity, and so forth.*

What Did We Do Before We Had Children?

This is a great question to ask each other. I bet that when you first met, you lingered and couldn't tear yourselves apart at the end of a date. You flirted, played, joked, and sexually teased. You also talked till the wee hours of the morning, texted through the day and night, wrote cute notes, and created fun surprises. Your relationship was your priority, and everything else came afterwards.

Somewhere along the way, there was courting, then living together or marriage. In the first year or two, you probably nurtured your relationship by making time for and caring about one another. You kissed, hugged, held hands, went on special outings and fun dates, made love on the living room floor or on a mountaintop. You made mad, passionate love by candlelight, took hot baths together, and wore sexy nightwear (or no nightwear whatsoever). Am I right?

Now that you are pregnant or already have a child, how much of that is still in place? If not, why did some of it diminish or outright go away? Do you blame your partner, or are you willing to take at least partial ownership of and responsibility for your part? What can *you* do to get the romance to return?

Create a Regular Dating Plan

I've already stated that "dating is not an option." If you want your marriage to flourish, you must spend time together. I have suggested to my clients that they create a four-week dating plan. Most people who implement the idea have found it to be fun and energizing. Here's a plan:

- *Week 1:* She plans something she knows he would like to do.
- *Week 2:* He plans something he knows she would like to do.
- *Week 3:* She plans something she would like to do.
- *Week 4:* He plans something he would like to do.

The person in charge of that week's activity gets the babysitter, makes the reservations, and does whatever is needed to have a special time together. The beautiful thing about this is that you both are engaged in a spirit of giving, you are both receiving, and you each get to do things you enjoy. You may not love going to the ballet or the hockey game, but you do it. Why? Because of love. Just remember, your dates don't have to cost a lot of money, and you can even stay at home after the children are in bed if you make adequate plans ahead of time.

Highs and Lows of Marriage

Marriages, just like individuals, have both highs and lows, good days and not so good days, joyous times and stressful periods. In his book *The Seven Principles for Making Marriage Work,* John Gottman says: "Happily married couples aren't smarter or more beautiful than others, and they don't live in castles in the clouds where there's no conflict or negative feelings. They've simply learned to let their positive feelings about each other override their negative ones."

If you think about it, that's a powerful concept and one well worth adopting. Badgering, criticizing, nagging, or complaining does not a happy relationship make.

Expectations

Another big problem that often occurs is having expectations that are not met. An expectation is a belief, hope, desire, probability, or assumption that something will occur. When it doesn't take place, people can become hurt, frustrated, angry, or even hostile. "I want my way, and I want it now" is the selfish expression of expectations.

Before getting married, my husband and I did a lengthy exercise about our hopes, desires, and expectations for one another and our partnership. That way, we created a firm foundation for how we wanted our lives to be. Neither of us wanted a repeat of what we had experienced in our prior marriages.

We also resolved many issues we thought might come up later. Some of the areas were: family, children, employment, religion, money management, intimacy, sexuality, in–laws, housekeeping/chores, home maintenance, friendships, and other significant topics.

The exercise has served us and my clients well, and I would be happy to share it with anyone who asks. In fact, it has been so successful that as my husband and I have reviewed it from time to time, we have had very little to alter. Any changes we wanted to make were discussed and negotiated lovingly. I believe that working things through early on helped to make the rest of our marriage run quite smoothly.

Having high, unrealistic, or even hidden expectations might be one of the most difficult of all marital problems. No one will ever meet all our needs and expectations, but if they are not adequately discussed, it can lead to a lot of disappointment and hurt. One remedy is *not having* expectations—which may be easier said than done. Or it might be lowering expectations. But the best solution is getting them out in the open, discussing them, and then coming up with solutions.

Exercise: List the categories that are important to each of you. You can look at some of the topics mentioned above. Take one at a time. Either write down your own desires and expectations and then share your lists together, or you can discuss each topic. It is a good idea to record your agreements so you have a roadmap.

> *The level of misery in a relationship can be correlated with the differences between reality and expectations.*
> —Unknown

Putting Your Head in the Sand

If you don't want to look at yourself—your patterns and behaviors—perhaps you are putting your head in the sand. Avoiding the truth is never profitable. So become aware of those troubles you don't want to examine. Determine the benefits of being honest with yourself, for they are many. Then look at what you may need or want to change in order to improve your life.

Sometimes, one person is upset about something, even the partnership, while the other thinks everything is fine just as it is. What's wrong with this picture? Somebody may be quite unaware of their partner's inner thoughts and attitudes. They haven't *stopped, looked, and listened*, which can lead to future conflict, heartache, and disappointment.

Self–Esteem

If your self–esteem is low, you might believe you are a failure. You may say, "I'm not good enough. I'm such a twit. What's wrong with me?" and other self–deprecating thoughts. The first step in having a happy marriage is being a happy, well–adjusted person. And truly, how many of us fit that category when we are first married, if ever? From our growing–up years, we carry a backpack of problems around with us—hurts, anger, discouragement, rejection, feeling that we're not good enough, and so forth—all of which affect our self–esteem, self–worth, and self–image.

One man I know continually blamed his parents for his crummy childhood. He believed his parents and siblings were the reason he consumed drugs and alcohol and made dysfunctional decisions throughout his life. On the other hand, his siblings were introspective, took responsibility for their actions, engaged in counseling, and were also able to forgive their parents, who they decided did the very best they knew how to do.

Building self–worth takes time, effort, and awareness. It also involves accepting, becoming content with, and discovering who you are. Though this can be a lifelong process, the benefits are many. You can lessen the load by understanding, expressing your needs, working through your issues, and perhaps engaging in counseling. You just may discover that inner beauty in yourself which I talked about earlier.

I have found that many people are unable to acknowledge the good things about themselves. It feels embarrassing, even arrogant. If you are lacking in a sense of self–worth, you can work on giving yourself praise, validation, and encouragement. Acknowledge your strengths, weaknesses, wants, needs, likes, dislikes, opinions, and judgments. Discover what you *do* like and approve of and recall positive occurrences. Visualize yourself succeeding.

Even if an audience of 10,000 is applauding and cheering, some people just don't believe they are good enough. Henry Ford made a brilliant statement: "Whether you think you can or think you can't, you are right."

The way you think controls your life. The mind pretty much believes what it is fed, so how about feeding it good food? No one else can make you happy. Happiness is an inside job.

Exercise: Take a piece of paper and make a list of all the things you excel at and are proud of, all your positive qualities, talents, gifts, and abilities. No one else needs to see it, so let it rip and think of everything you can without judgment. This is not an ego trip; it is just a way to acknowledge your true self, so be honest. Then look at your list frequently to remind yourself of the awesome person you truly are. I hope the list is long.

You will be as loving in your relationship
as you are loving to yourself.
So make that part of your life's work.

Cognitive Distortions—Tell the Truth

Everyone does *self–talk* throughout the day. Much of the time, however, it is negative, unsupportive, or even illogical. At other times, it is positive, supportive, and generous. Since our thoughts are always present, why not focus on the positive, which is more often than not the truth?

Exercise: Take a piece of paper and draw a line down the center. On the left side, write **Negative Things I Say**. List one negative, irrational, unsupportive, or self–defeating thought you have about yourself. On the right side, write **Positive Things I Could Say** and list all the positive, supportive, rational, self–embracing, and truthful statements. It's important to *tell the truth* about yourself instead of lingering on the illogical or self–defeating aspects. This exercise won't heal all the wounds, but it will allow you to see what is actually accurate and can help train your mind to look at your life in a more productive manner.

Negative, Irrational, Unsupportive, Self–Defeating Statements	***Positive, Supportive, Rational, Self–Embracing, Truthful Statements***
Example: I am not very smart.	I got A's in high school as well as in college.
	I have a degree and am successful in my job.
	I figure things out easily and know where to look for answers.
	I've been told I'm very good at _____.
	Etc.

The Magic Question

This is a very valuable exercise, as it encourages you to take responsibility for your part in your relationship. Use the contemplation skill first and look at what YOU would be doing if you woke up tomorrow morning and *magically* everything was wonderful, just the way you wanted things to be.

While there may be a temptation to think that external events or other individuals, such as your partner, should change, I challenge you to think only about what YOU can do to make a difference.

Exercise: So here is the magic question to contemplate: "If I woke up tomorrow morning and suddenly everything was magically wonderful, just the way I wanted it to be, what would *I* be doing to make it so?" Write down everything you can think of and include effective behaviors you are presently doing; also examine other attitudes and actions that would improve your lives.

Keep in mind what your partner has told you he or she would like from you, whether said when calm or frustrated. As already shown, one person can change a relationship in dramatic ways. If she starts being more affectionate, he may be more attentive. If he takes her out on more dates or spends more time communicating, she might be more responsive physically. Be specific and write as many ideas as you can think of that already work well, and also what *you* can do to improve your marriage.

Mending Your Marriage

This means being willing and able to find effective ways to fix negative interactions, damages, or hurts that may occur. According to John Gottman, 69% of a couple's conflicts are perpetual issues that don't go away and involve both personality and lifestyle needs. If not discussed, the disagreements can lead to gridlock, which can lead to emotional distancing. However, even if there is no agreement, acceptance, humor, and a good–natured spirit about the differences can be attempted. The other 31% of problems can probably be worked through. So allow positive feelings to override negative ones. These lyrics sung by many well–known singers say it well:

> *Accentuate the positive,*
> *Eliminate the negative,*
> *Latch on to the affirmative,*
> *But don't mess with mister in–between.*

In the end, most of our perceived big problems are really small issues. So mend the things you can and accept the things you can't. You can't change anyone unless they want to change. You can only change yourself, so here are some steps:

- *Notice that something is wrong.* You may not agree, but if something is off kilter for one partner, it will be off in some way for both. So acknowledge that there is an issue, even if you disagree.
- *Seek to understand* one another's feelings about the matter through effective dialogue, using good communication skills.
- *Solve the issue,* but only after there is good understanding on both sides. Ask for what is needed and make reasonable requests.

- *Identify the cause* if you can. It is usually best to wait until things have calmed down. This can be challenging but very useful if you don't want the situation to repeat itself.
- *Implement the solutions* that seem the most viable.
- *Evaluate the situation.* Come back together to continue the discussion as needed.
- A*gree to disagree.* Sometimes this is best. Do it calmly, and don't keep bringing it up.

Attitude

Be aware of your attitude. Is it positive or negative, optimistic or pessimistic? Notice which works best. Thoughts come and go like little thieves in the night. They can catch you unaware; but once they appear and you notice they are there, you can change them. While you can't always change your circumstances or what happens in the moment, you *can* change your attitude.

Sometimes it can be helpful to "act as if." For example, act as if you have confidence. "Fake it till you make it" may seem phony, but don't you feel better? Think about times you have gone to work or out in public when you were depressed or unhappy. You faked it, perhaps because you didn't want others to see your bad mood. You soon forgot about what was bothering you and became happier, right? If the feelings persist, go back and figure it out.

Awareness Brings Choice—ABC

Sometimes people have a certain feeling. They let it rule the day and remain on automatic. For example, if you wake up depressed, you may continue on autopilot without acknowledging what you are feeling. You may be grumpy to your family, want to stay in bed for the day, or feel sorry for yourself. However, if you *stop and look* you will *notice* that you are depressed and might even be able to chase down the reason.

Imagine a light bulb and let that represent awareness of the feeling or attitude. When the light bulb is on, awareness is present. At that point, consider your options to change your feelings. I call this **Awareness Brings Choice**, or **ABC.** You might choose to stay with your thoughts, or you can check out your options and do something different. Although you can't avoid having a feeling that suddenly comes upon you, you can change how you respond to it. Options are always available.

A = Awareness. When you are aware, you are conscious and awake. You see the truth and can choose to either change something or go along with it.

B = Brings or creates an opportunity for...

C = Choice. For example, instead of remaining depressed, you could distract yourself, reframe things, look for the bright side, go for a walk, make a therapy appointment, call a friend, read a book, paint a picture, or... It's okay if you consciously choose to remain with your mood, but be aware that you are doing so. Imagine a recent negative feeling and make a list of the possible options/choices you might have selected. Again, if the feeling persists, look at it and see the root and what you can change.

Feelings

I was in a relationship once where I was told my feelings were wrong. I said, "No, they are just my feelings. If I acted on them in a negative way, such as screaming or hitting, I would be wrong; but my feelings are my feelings, and I'm entitled to feel how I feel." And so are you! This did not go over very well, but fortunately I stood my ground. Your feelings are never wrong. However, the way you say or handle your feelings may not be beneficial to you or to the situation. Again, you can make effective or ineffective choices. Which works best?

Empathy

Empathy means being aware of another's feelings and emotions. It's an ability to almost place yourself in another's shoes and feel understanding and compassion for what they are experiencing. Empathy most certainly promotes closeness, because you connect with something within them and can express kindness. Some effective words might be, "I don't know what to say, but I'm so glad you told me about it." Or, "That must feel awful for you. I feel sad that you are experiencing this." Empathy is best described as feeling with someone, understanding them, getting in their shoes, and imagining what it would be like. You don't have to have experienced something similar, but it may help if you have.

Sympathy and empathy are close cousins, but sympathy is like pity. It acknowledges that you don't feel the same but will try to understand. Some sympathetic replies are, "Oh, you poor thing. That's the worst thing I've ever heard. No wonder you are in the dumps so much." To some, sympathy can create disconnection.

How would you feel if you heard this comment? "I'm sorry you lost the baby, but at least you have two children already." Or, "Well, you can just get another dog." These statements are not comforting at all. Sympathy implies that people are alone and just need to cope by themselves, while empathy is nurturing and comforting.

When couples understand and have empathy toward one another, they are tolerant, forgiving, kind, and accepting. Just use good listening skills without attempting to offer solutions. "That sounds tough for you; I feel so sad for you; I'm here for you" will provide empathy and support, which is usually what is needed. Sometimes, just a listening ear with a feeling of compassion radiating forth is all anyone really wants.

Ask, "I'd love to do something for you. What would be helpful?" Or you can just take the reins and *do* something supportive, like making a special meal or shoveling the walk without being asked. Reflecting the feeling/essence or asking pertinent and non–judgmental questions will also be appreciated

Love Is Spelled T I M E

You don't have to spend a lot of money to go on dates, enjoy activities, have fun, and share laughter. Be present personally for important events and be available mentally, physically, and emotionally. If your love is waning or you don't feel the love you once felt, do your part to rebuild it. Remember, sometimes just a small gesture can yield big results.

Make up your own words to stand for Love and Time, such as:

T = togetherness
I = intimacy
M = meaningfulness
E = empathy

Toilet Paper and Other Small Stuff

What does toilet paper (TP) have to do with anything? It's just an example of how small, unimportant annoyances can cause horrific distress.

> *Cherise and Sam were clients who were contemplating divorce. One of their main issues was the fact that Sam never put the new toilet paper on the bar when the old roll was gone. He left the new one on the floor for Cherise to place on the bar. She would get furious and complain that Sam never did anything for her, that everything was left up to her, and that he was the most selfish person in the world. No matter what we talked about or what interventions we did, Sam didn't change his toilet paper and other "selfish" ways; and Cherise continued to badger him.*

Just as we were making a little progress, they dropped out of counseling. This happens sometimes when people don't want to face their problems. They both said their relationship was too far gone to repair. Unfortunately, they couldn't or wouldn't alter their underlying issue of blame and disrespect instead of taking responsibility and performing acts of love. My guess is that they divorced over their many small irritations instead of caring enough to treat one another with admiration, love, and regard.

Here's a happier toilet paper story. When my husband and I got married, I found that he always put the toilet paper on the bar with the end coming from underneath. Personally I liked the end on the top, and my family had always done it that way. Oh, yes, and this included how we placed the paper towel on the towel bar, as well.

One time, a dear friend visited, and we were joking about the "right" and most "scientifically correct" way to situate the paper towel. It became a long and "very serious" discussion. To illustrate my point that *over* was better, I went to the pantry door and barely touched the roll that was coming from *underneath*. To my surprise, it began to unravel without stopping. Much to my delight, it proved my point, and it took quite a while to get our hysterical laughter under control.

You might say I learned to pick my battles because I cooperatively let the TP come from underneath all these years. Not a topic to lose our equanimity over. Yes, I gave in, but it really was no big deal for me. I can stand up if something is important.

People fight over the smallest problems—the toilet seat left up, the toothpaste cap never closed, how to prepare spaghetti the right way, who didn't put gas in the car, blah, blah, blah. Really! Couples argue over the tiniest issues. Of course, repetitive small occurrences add up, I agree. But as Nike says, "Just Do It." Care about one another enough to be kind and thoughtful. There are bigger problems in your lives, so "Don't sweat the small stuff." That's my motto.

The Relative Scale of Importance

The following exercise will help you see the relative importance/non–importance of things in your life. If you keep the value of each negative event in mind, you will learn to place attention on what really matters. It will also help you to avoid exhausting your energy on a small issue. Consider a problem you've had and how much value you've given it. Then look at how much energy you expended. You might see that you have used $80 worth of energy on a very small matter.

Exercise: Make a list of *problems* that could occur or have already occurred in your lives. Give each one a number indicating their relative importance on a scale of $1 to $100. A $100 problem may be that someone close to you just died. A $90 problem may be that someone you love has been diagnosed with a terminal illness. A $50 problem may be that you totaled your car and had some injuries but you will be all right. A $1 problem may be that someone left their shoes in the front hall. Keep in mind that some matters, such as those shoes, can add up if done day after day.

Next, suppose you only have $100 worth of *energy* in a day. Look at the amount of energy you have expended on trivial problems in the past. A $5 problem only deserves $5 worth of energy, not $75 (which could happen if you argued, criticized, blamed, etc.). Really, now, how big is the fact that he forgot to pick up milk, especially if he is willing to go to the store and correct his error? It's no wonder you run out of oomph by the end of the day when you give excessive energy to a small problem.

Problem:

$1 – –– – – – –– – – – – – – $50 – – – – – – – – – – $100

Energy Expended:

$1 – –– – – – –– – – – – – – $50 – – – – – – – – – – $100

7 Keys to Your Sweetheart's Heart: What Partners Need to Feel Most Loved

One of the biggest problems I have found in marriage, and other relationships, too, including children, is that people don't understand other's needs, wants, and desires. He may think that she loves receiving flowers, but what she really wants is to spend quality time together, perhaps snuggling by the fire or taking moonlight walks. She thinks he will appreciate how well she cleaned the house or that she texts love messages to him at work seven times a day. What he really wants is more sexual intimacy or her appreciation for the great remodeling job he is doing in the basement.

Assumptions can be inaccurate. Receivers may not feel cared about because their *most important needs* are not being met, while givers may feel they can *never do enough*. However, the problem is that they are simply not using the *right keys* to unlock the door of the heart.

If you really want to be loving, strive to see things through your partner's eyes by learning the *primary keys* to meet his or her needs. When you do, magical things can happen. Caution! Don't stop doing the other nice things, too; just recognize that if you do what is really meaningful, you will put more money in the Relationship Bank Account (described below).

Exercise: Individually, look at the seven topics and select the ones that are most important to you. Choose your top two or three, then write down the *specific* things you would appreciate your partner doing in these categories. (It is equally appropriate to do this for/with your children, too.)

The 7 Keys

Presents—Give surprises, gifts, flowers, cards, sweet notes left in a suitcase or love messages on the bathroom mirror. Do the unexpected, other than just giving gifts at Christmas, on birthdays, or on Valentine's Day. Give freely all the time. There are lots of ways to give.

Also consider *presence*—being there, being present, being available, not distracted.

Affection—Share hugs, kisses, squeezes, hand holding, pats. Help me feel close and connected to you through kind and appropriate physical touching.

Appreciation—Give me acknowledgment, praise, validation, affirmation, and thanks. Really see me and know me. Provide encouragement, assurance, and support.

Communication—Share your thoughts and feelings with me. Talk to me about you. Be a good listener. Hear and care about what I am saying.

Create safety when I express my feelings. Be willing to resolve conflict. We can learn and practice effective communication skills.

Time Together—Spend time with me doing things we both enjoy. Realize that just *being* together is more important than *what* we are doing. Let's go out on dates. Sometimes we can be in the same environment doing separate things but still feel joined.

Selfless Service—Perform loving acts of kindness and do nice things without complaining or keeping a tally. Accomplish tasks without my asking. Open doors for me or make meals I love. Divide chores with me and follow through on commitments in a timely way. Do things you know I would appreciate. Help to manage my and our commitments and expectations.

Sexual Intimacy—Ask me what I need and want sexually. Please do some of the foreplay I love. Respect, enjoy, and love my body and make me feel desired and desirable. Make certain we both get our needs met much of the time.

This is a powerful exercise! To help you remember this concept, think of the word **PACTS**, spelled **PAACTSS** (see the seven bolded words above). When you have both completed the exercise, discuss the categories you noted with your partner and share them in the order of importance. Then reveal the *specific things* each of you would like your partner to do for you in those areas.

Make copies of what you wrote and share them so you can implement the meaningful behaviors that will be most appreciated. Make a PACT with yourself to do some of those things every day. I guarantee that this will foster the maximum effective demonstrations of love and caring and will enhance your relationship more than you might imagine.

> *The deepest principle of human nature is the craving to be appreciated.*
> —William James, psychologist

Be the Go–To Person

In a good marriage, each partner usually wants to be the "go-to" person when something needs to be shared. If you have a loving and supportive relationship, your spouse will be the one with whom you most want to communicate your joys and sorrows, your wins and losses, your accomplishments and challenges.

If that is not so, what do you need to learn about him or her and then put into practice? One of the best ways to discover what is most needed and wanted and then provide it is to do the above exercise. To be a bit personal, my most important key is Affection—holding hands, warm hugs out of the blue, snuggling, spontaneous kisses, and kisses when we leave and return. It means so much to me when my husband meets this need and my other important needs. And I know it means a lot to him when I meet his most important needs, one of the main ones being Appreciation.

Most people love to be appreciated, praised, validated, affirmed, complimented, and provided with encouragement and support. Even if that's not a primary key for you or your partner, it is still an exceedingly valuable part of a relationship. When a person feels valued and important, they will be willing to meet you more than halfway with most of your wants and desires. You will also be the person with whom they most want to share. And this is a good recipe for that loving and passionate marriage that I hope you are seeking.

Personal Responsibility

Taking responsibility means accepting ownership for your behaviors as well as the consequences that follow. Everyone makes mistakes and poor choices; so owning up at the outset is the wise and responsible thing to do. Saying "I didn't do that" if you actually did just creates ill feelings and distrust. You can only change what you are aware of and what you decide to take responsibility for. It is truly empowering to take personal responsibility.

Another aspect of responsibility is being aware of what is needed and acting on it: You notice that the baby needs to be changed, the neighbor's sidewalk needs to be shoveled, or the neighborhood park could benefit from someone picking up the trash. It's so meaningful when someone does these things just to be kind and cooperative rather than after they're cajoled or coerced.

In a marriage, both parties need to take responsibility for their actions and reactions each and every day. Being irresponsible will catch up with you one day and may cause you to devalue yourself or create problems in your relationship.

When I counsel a woman (or man) who is being dominated, I always ask what her role has been in creating the problem. She seldom has an answer. Her part probably was that she was passive and allowed it to happen, or she didn't know what to do. When she understands her role or takes responsibility for her part, she can decide to leave things as they are or make meaningful changes.

If you don't acknowledge your role, you may become a victim and believe you are helpless. But if you take responsibility for your part, however small it may be, you can have some control of the situation—and it feels good, too.

Dominant/Submissive Pattern

I have seen the dominance and submission dance in my practice so much that I can say it is one of the more prominent models of unhappiness in couples. Sometimes it is a man who feels controlled or dominated, but more often it is a woman. The pattern may begin because one or the other wants to please, to be happy, or be congenial; and they believe the only way to do so is to "go along with" the dominant partner. The other person may have been used to getting his or her way and expects to, and when allowed, he or she simply keeps the controlling actions going.

Always remember that we teach people how to treat us. The longer a pattern persists, the longer it will take to change—that is, if the other person is even willing to make a change. The woman who has been dominated must figure out that she has *allowed herself* to be dominated. When she takes responsibility, then she has choice—a choice to disallow the dynamic, discuss the matter, find a counselor, leave, etc. (And of course this is also true if the submissive person is a man.) Ask for what you want, be lovingly open, but stand your ground if someone is being disrespectful.

After years and years of assuming control, the one dominating his or her spouse may not be open to change.

The dominator can choose to make the marriage work by changing himself/herself or continuing in the same pattern. Indeed, both parties have choice and the power to change the situation. It's best to nip this dynamic in the bud because it usually backfires at some point. It behooves couples to avoid these tendencies and be on guard for dominant and submissive tendencies early on. Such behavior can be terribly abusive.

Estelle was a beautiful 48-year-old woman who had been with her husband, Herb, for over 10 years. He told her what to do and when, he criticized most of her actions, and he constantly belittled her, even in front of others. Whenever she confronted him, even gently, he became angry; he would shut down and wouldn't speak to her for days. She learned to stuff her feelings and put up with his negative behaviors.

He had told her to "get out" so many times that she finally took him up on his request and left. However, after a few weeks, he apologized, as he had often done, and she moved back home. He was nice for a few days but then reverted to his former behavior. When she couldn't take it any longer, she moved to an apartment and then came to see me. They had been separated several times, but she seemed serious on this occasion.

During one of our sessions, I asked her why she seemed so attached to him. She struggled to answer the question, but some of the reasons were: "He gives me financial security, he takes care of a lot of things, and he is a father to my son, even though he's mean to him, too, at times. We have a nice house, and I'm lonely without him." Then I queried, "So it sounds like all of those things are more valuable to you than the negative aspects about how treats you?" She pondered and then said, "Oh, my. I guess so. Those are not very good reasons, are they?"

The end of the story isn't important for this purpose. The important thing was that Herb had no intention of changing and found ways to blame Estelle for everything he didn't like. His haranguing made her feel worthless and insignificant. Her big decision was to decide if she wanted to live with someone who continually demeaned her, even though there were other beneficial parts to the relationship, or leave him for the unknown. Sometimes, immense growth and development can come from taking a leap of faith when there is no hope for change, especially if one is being abused.

Boundary Setting

If a dominant/submissive pattern exists, the one who is being dominated needs to set boundaries. This is a very difficult task because the dominator wants to maintain control and believes that he (for the purpose of this example) can and should be able to say and do whatever he desires. Boundaries are hard to set with adults because we fear how they will be received. But if consequences and limits are not implemented, the same behaviors will continue as in the dominant/submissive pattern above.

One of my clients has been afraid to say she is displeased with the verbal abuse she regularly receives because she is afraid her boyfriend won't talk to her for days and days (which has happened), or that he will get even angrier. She regrets ever standing up to him and just takes the abuse. "He won't change his behavior, and he won't talk anything through with me, so why bother?" Maybe she is in the wrong relationship.

For example, it won't be effective for her to cry because she is so hurt, or say, "Don't you ever talk to me like that again!" because she has probably said that over and over with no change. Instead, she might say, "Your yelling at me is unacceptable. I am leaving for a while until you/we can speak respectfully." Using "we" is less caustic but may not be as effective. Blame is sometimes well–deserved if one is abusive.

Some boundary setting can sound harsh, but nothing will change if you accept the same behaviors over and over. The consequence should be something you are willing and able to carry out. If you don't follow through, you will not be believed, and leverage has been lost. Empty threats never work. You may not change the other person, but you can do something for yourself.

Self and child protection are critical. Limits need to be established assertively, not in an angry or hostile way. Humiliating or punitive consequences are ineffective and demeaning, which is not the purpose.

It is much easier to set boundaries with children, and this must be done or they will believe they can do what they want. It is more challenging to do with a spouse, especially if one is particularly passive. The idea of setting boundaries is to help the dominator recognize that the controlling behavior is not acceptable or will no longer work. It is not about *changing* them; it is about *respecting and protecting* the person who is being controlled.

Selfish or Selfless

Abigail Van Buren wisely said: "There are two kinds of people in the world—those who walk into a room and say, 'There you are,' and those who say, 'Here I am!'" Which one are you? Are you interested in others, or are you focused on yourself?

> *Several years ago, a couple was involved in my "Marriage Success Program" for engaged and newly married couples. No matter what was presented, one of the brides-to-be acted totally self-centered. She wanted things the way she wanted them and seemed unequivocally bent on having her own way. Nothing we discussed unraveled her selfish habits. Even the numerous skills and exercises did not assuage her self-centeredness. She and her fiancé quarreled constantly, and they didn't appear to understand the basics of love. I will always wonder if they ever got married, and if they did, whether they could have been happy. Education is a powerful thing, but people must be willing to learn and grow.*

A selfish person is concerned primarily for herself, regardless of others' needs or wants. She usually talks about herself, serves her own needs, and neglects what might be beneficial or agreeable to others. If you want your own way and are unwilling to compromise, negotiate, or let go, you will not create an environment of love and caring.

The Gift of Time Off

Everyone deserves a break. When it is feasible, you can adopt a policy where each of you has a night completely free of evening meal preparation, being with the kids, and putting them to bed. You are off duty. You could pick one day a week that is typically unstructured for one of you so the other can attend a class, go to a movie, or just sit in the bedroom and read with no interruptions. The other parent is in charge of the family. During the same week, that other parent would be given the same gift.

You can execute this idea more frequently or less often. In prescribing this to my clients, they have loved the idea of being totally free of responsibility for one evening each week. Best of all, they learn not to keep score. They do things lovingly and unselfishly for the sake of the children and each other.

Another idea is to use the weekend to let each parent have one morning to sleep in with no responsibilities until early afternoon. I realize that work schedules, meetings, and life happen, but you can experiment and find a structure that will work for you.

Exercise: Create a schedule for time off. Try it for a few weeks and see if it works for you.

The Relationship Bank Account

Whether people know it or not, they are always creating a Relationship Bank Account. Just like real banks, they place both deposits and withdrawals into their relationship. Deposits can be thought of as kind, considerate, generous, good–will promoting words or actions. Withdrawals can be thought of as unkind, inconsiderate, selfish, aggressive, disrespectful, or ill-willed words or actions.

The difference is that in a regular financial account, the exchange is $1 for $1. In the Relationship Bank Account, it takes at least five deposits or $5 to make up for one withdrawal, or $5 to $1. In my experience, it is more like 20 deposits to equal one withdrawal, or $20 to $1. Keep well in mind that it will take time and effort to build the account back up again.

It's no wonder that people get in the red very quickly. The clients in my practice who are troubled have many withdrawals and few deposits, or they may even be in the hole. However, the ones who have used this concept learn to be more conscious about what they say and do in order to create abundant deposits to increase their assets.

Exercise: Each of you take out a sheet of paper and draw a line down the middle. On one side write Deposits, and on the other side write Withdrawals. Make a list of things you do or might do to generate Deposits and Withdrawals in your partner's account. Then make a list of things your partner does or might do to generate Deposits and Withdrawals in your account. Share your lists and discuss where you can each improve. Respect each other's feelings and don't argue. How many deposits do you have in your account?

Apologizing

> *The first to apologize is the bravest. The first to forgive is the strongest. The first to forget is the happiest.*
> —Unknown

Since human beings are not perfect, they occasionally say and do things they are not proud of. "I'm sorry" can be difficult for some people to express. However, they are two of the most important words one can ever verbalize. Saying "I'm sorry" but continuing to do the same thing over and over is ineffective and destructive. It is critical to offer apologies with sincerity and make every effort not to repeat the offense.

When your partner is working to avoid doing what offended you, consider giving a bit of slack, since change can take time. And don't hesitate to ask for forbearance when you are in the same boat. Both sides can show forgiveness and generosity and give one another the benefit of the doubt.

Here are four steps for apologizing:

1. Say, *"I'm sorry for ___."* Be specific about what *you* did or said, not that you are sorry they feel that way or are sorry they took it wrong. Focus on your own behaviors.
2. Show you understand that what you said may have been wrong or hurt the other's feelings. *"I know I hurt your feelings/made you feel bad when I ..."*
3. State what you will do in the future. Keep the language positive as to what you *will do*, versus what you *won't do*. For example, *"In the future I will _____."* Do whatever is the right thing for that circumstance. Be specific.
4. Ask for forgiveness. *"Will you/can you forgive me?"* or *"Please forgive me."*
5. Do your best never to repeat the offense.

A happy marriage is the union of two good forgivers.
—Robert Quille

Forgiveness

Asking for forgiveness is as important as apologizing. It means intentionally changing feelings and attitudes toward a person who has caused harm, offended, or hurt you. Empathy, compassion, and understanding should also be present.

Forgiving another does not mean that you condone the words or actions or minimize what was done. But you can forgive the person without excusing the act.

> *Isabelle said, "It took two years, but I finally forgave Milton for having the affair. I held onto the anger for so long, it was hurting me more than it was hurting him. When I released all of that, I forgave his actions in my own heart, even though I was unable to tell him directly at the time. I felt so much better and was able to move forward. Eventually, we talked about it all and healed our marriage. I can now admit that I was as much to blame for making us miserable as he was. It's a wonder he stuck around."*

Letting go of pent–up feelings, anger, and resentment is key to *your* happiness and well–being as well as the other person's. It is also beneficial to look at what part you may have played in the situation, however small. You can be humble and ask forgiveness if you had any culpability in the situation whatsoever.

Plan Interesting Adventures

Ask your sweetheart to pack a suitcase with certain appropriate items, and then go on an unexpected trip (car, plane, train, or whatever). Make it a total surprise. Surprises are such fun for most people.

Plan and execute unusual dates and outings. You could make a list of things you would like to do and share your ideas. Pull them out when you need a surprise or seem at a loss for how to keep life interesting. Don't forget to bring in a bit of romance, as well.

You could do this for any holiday or birthday, or for another occasion. Just make it fun and inviting—and romantic. Angela wrote about her Valentine adventure:

This Valentine's Day, I created a treasure hunt around the house for my husband. Each clue had a promise for a surprise and also gave a hint for finding the next clue. The poems were perhaps a bit hokey, but he loved searching around and figuring out the clues. We had a wonderful evening. And it led to some fun adult activities after the kids went to sleep.

Affection

Do you hold hands in a movie, or sit with your arms in your own lap? Do you sit on the couch together and snuggle when watching TV at home, or do you sit in separate chairs? Do you spend time together, or go your separate ways after dinner? How about finding ways to be companions? The dishes, email, or laundry won't go away, will they?

Do you ever just go up to her when she is fixing dinner, give her a hug, and whisper sweet nothings in her ear? Do you ever give him a brief shoulder rub and say, "I love you so much" while he's rocking the baby? And how about a special hug or pat on the back to your child, along with a statement of gratitude for a job well done?

Pats, teases, smiles, hugs, and saying "I love you" every day will put deposits into your relationship bank account, as will compliments and other gestures of affection. Did you know that 12 ten-second hugs a day keep the therapist away? So how much time does that take out of your day? Hmm, 120 seconds is just two minutes. Can you spare that much—even a lot more—to show love to your spouse and your children?

Laughter and Humor

Laughter and humor can get you out of lots of jams. Nothing works faster to lift your burdens and bring you back to balance, and they can work wonders to lighten the air and enhance your relationship.

Norman Cousins was an American political journalist, author, professor, and world peace advocate. In 1964 he had a serious illness and was given a 1 in 500 chance of living. He didn't buy into his prognosis and did three things: 1. He fired his doctor. 2. He got massive doses of vitamin C. 3. He found a movie projector and a pile of funny movies, which he watched. He laughed so hard that his stomach hurt, but he lived 26 years longer than he was projected to live. Perhaps it can't be proven that it was humor that increased his life, but it did strengthen his immune system.

Humor is the antidote for stress, pain, and illness because it helps to heal the body by releasing endorphins and boosting the immune system. Joke books, comic strips, fun movies, and clips on YouTube can bring gales of laughter. Teasing respectfully makes difficulties and tensions dissipate quickly but should never be used to deliver jabs, sarcasm, or disrespect.

Acts of Kindness

Even after all this time the sun never says to the earth, 'You owe me.' Look what happens with a love like that. It lights the whole sky.
—Hafiz

Some couples only think to celebrate obligatory events, such as birthdays, Valentine's Day, Christmas, and anniversaries. Others come to *expect* continual repetition of kind deeds that are done out of the goodness of the heart. But it is the daily moments and acts of kindness, often spontaneous, that are most meaningful. Sweet, simple acts of kindness and unselfish service go a long way. Expecting that something once done should be continued takes away the aspect of generous giving. Let people do things out of love, not out of obligation.

Surprises are also rewarding. My husband still talks about the day I left him a note to meet me after work up the mountainside across from our house. I had made a picnic supper and ran up ahead of him to set things up. Just before he left home, it started to rain. Knowing our summer rains could be very brief, he brought a poncho to keep us dry. Sure enough, the sun came out 15 minutes later and we had a delightful picnic—and he loved the surprise!

Exercise: Create a list of what you know *your partner would like you to do,* and another list of what *you would enjoy your partner doing* with and for you. Share your lists, if you like. Do not expect all of it to be done. Use the lists as guidelines to inform, encourage, and sparkle up your lives.

How to Treat Your Most Important Person

Over time, some couples abandon or forget to do the things they did early on for that most important person. When such things are neglected, life can become dull and humdrum.

The movie *Hope Springs* is about an older couple. The wife, played by Meryl Streep, is unhappy and feels taken for granted because the romance with her husband, played by Tommy Lee Jones, has disappeared. She is intent on getting it back. His usual habit is to shout hello or goodbye or give her a hasty peck on the cheek. She complains that all intimacy and any show of caring have completely vanished. She tries to get him to go for marital therapy. He resists, but she persists. I highly recommend the movie. It is humorous and illustrates in a fun, interesting, and informative way how they were able to reignite their spark of love and romance.

One of my clients shared with me how she and her children treat their most important person—her husband and their father.

Whenever Ed comes home from work, the children and I totally stop what we are doing, whether it's fixing dinner, playing a game, or watching a TV show. We all run to the door to shower hugs and load him with attention. He loves it and feels so happy, even after a tough day at the office. It also helps teach the children that relationships are the most important thing. The kids have learned to do this for me, too, and it has created a beautiful closeness in our family.

And here's another story:

Fred always makes me feel as though I am the most important person in the world. He listens to me talk about my tiring day with the kids. He rubs my shoulders, helps with dinner, and makes a fire in the fireplace on cold evenings. I know I am more important than sports, TV, washing the car, or talking to colleagues. If I need or want him, he is there for me. I feel so very lucky. Most of my friends aren't so fortunate.

Simply Being Still

It can be challenging, especially with a new baby and/or other children, to find time just to be, to be still, or to be quiet. Nothing will make you feel more peaceful, relaxed, and nurtured than taking 10 or 15 minutes out of your busy day just to be still. Try doing this several times a day when you are able. You will gain more aliveness and energy afterwards and might accomplish extra tasks. It will also help you become more focused and calm over time.

Whether you call this meditation, being quiet, contemplation, or whatever, the intent is to try to quiet your mind. When thoughts arise, do not judge them; simply be aware of them and return to your practice. The goal is to learn to be present, here in the moment.

There are a number of things you can do to be still, so choose what works for you. Focus on your breath, breathing slowly in and out; say a simple word over and over, such as peace, love, or some short phrase. On your in–breath, focus on bringing in love, nurturing, positive messages; on the out–breath, focus on letting go of stress, tension, negativity. When you become aware of intruding thoughts, simply go back to what you were doing, and let the thoughts go by. There are many other techniques, so if you are interested, you can look them up online.

Attitude of Gratitude

Everything is a gift of the universe—even joy, anger, jealousy, frustration or separateness. Everything is perfect, either for our growth or our enjoyment.
—Ken Keyes, Jr.

The word *gratitude* stems from the Latin word *gratia*, which means grace, graciousness, thankfulness, appreciation. There is a definite connection between gratitude and well–being. It can improve attitudes, heart health, and immune systems, and can surely decrease stress. Friendships and close relationships are upgraded because people enjoy being around positive and gracious individuals. Even seeing or experiencing negative events increases thankfulness. Think of how gratitude amplified after the terrible events of September 11, 2001. Sadly, the memory of that time has diminished and so have some of the gratitude and service.

Some ways to express gratitude are to sit for a few minutes each day and recount those things for which you are thankful. Thank–you notes, verbal expressions of appreciation, mindfulness meditation, and keeping a gratitude journal are also ways of keeping gratitude in your heart. If you keep a gratitude journal, you can write each day about things you are grateful for. Finding a time that regularly works for you will create a habit and become part of your everyday thinking. It's fun to go back and read, especially when you have a sad or funky day. Those clients who have followed this advice or have sat for five to ten minutes each day focusing on thankfulness have developed a more optimistic attitude about life and their relationships.

Simply sharing your appreciation with others for something done or said works wonders. Everyone wants to be seen, and gratitude is a way of noticing others for who they are and what they do. We can also be grateful for those seen and unseen miracles from God, or whatever one believes in—for the earth, sun, rain, gravity, nature, abilities, talents, family members, and life itself.

It is especially meaningful to show appreciation to our partners and children. So often, people focus on what is wrong in the relationship. That negativity feeds on itself over and over. But focusing on the positive things absolutely creates a more loving, compassionate, and optimistic attitude. So do it often for others; and do it for you, as well.

Spirituality and Religion

Of course, not everyone is religious or spiritual, and no one can force their views upon others, nor should they; but as you look beyond yourself for sustenance, it can make life more enriching, comforting, and meaningful. While many people don't claim to be religious, many are spiritual. They believe in something greater than themselves and may express it through yoga, prayer, meditation, personal reflection, contemplation, or service. Others attend churches, synagogues, or mosques, and many pray and study together.

It has been said that, generally speaking, spiritual and religious people have a greater sense of meaning and purpose for their lives. They may be more curious about why they are here, what they are here to do, and where they may be going. On the other hand, it is not fair to badger, convert, or guilt a person into your beliefs. Sustain, support, and reinforce that which is dear to others simply out of love and respect, even though you don't participate directly.

It's also said that spiritual and religious people have greater optimism, more positive relationships, and are more nurturing and compassionate. They may be happier and have greater commitment to their relationships or to a cause. Certainly there are many wonderful people who are not religious or spiritual and who also do the above things; but religion and spirituality do add another dimension to life.

Even if you and your spouse or partner are not of the same religion or belief system, it will be appreciated if you offer support to each other. You might attend church, go to lectures, meditate, or celebrate religious holidays together as a couple and as a family. Praying together can be a powerful show of gratitude, love, and support. Gratitude to God or toward whatever you believe in, and gratitude for each other, will improve your life and help you maintain harmony, intimacy, and a loving connection.

A Final Word

Have I said often enough that life will not always be joyous? There will naturally be ups and downs, joys and sorrows, satisfaction and disappointment, health and illness, happiness and sadness, and even tragedy. Those things are just part of life, but they can be managed. No matter how challenging existence becomes, how exhausting, or how much you long to escape to a far–off island, it is all worth it.

The compensation for a happy marriage and effective parenting is immense. Through your example and willingness to overcome obstacles and challenges, you can be a light to your family, as well as to others in your life and in your sphere of influence.

Though it may seem difficult now, you may never know how much you have impacted your children by having a loving relationship. One day, they will appreciate your efforts and dedication toward creating a happy home for your family, and it will be their legacy to pass along to their own families.

I encourage you to enjoy your children while they are young. Sometimes it seems they will never grow up; but when they are gone, you will realize that the years flew past at a tremendous pace, and you will wish you could have some of that time back. That is certainly how I feel. Those were wonderful and precious times. I often wish I could go back in time, even for a few special moments. However, I will forever cherish the many beautiful memories we have had and continue to have together. New circumstances arrive and life is precious later on, too; I can assure you of that. I wouldn't trade my growing family for anything.

If every couple who wants to have a family would make themselves aware of some of the dangers and pitfalls, as well as the immense possibilities for joy and happiness, I believe they could avert many problems before they arise.

Prospective parents tend to focus on how to take care of their baby but not on how to nurture their precious relationships. And so I hope this book has been helpful to you in strengthening your marriage while raising a family. If so, please give a copy of the book or the e-book to your family, children, siblings, friends, or anyone you know who has children or is having a baby. I also believe many of the ideas will be helpful to marriages, whether the couples have children or not.

It is my personal belief that all circumstances, however arduous they might be, are gifts. Those who learn from their misfortunes and problems grow immensely as individuals and will develop as partners by holding one another close—physically, mentally, emotionally, and spiritually. Many worthwhile and essential lessons are derived from adversities.

When in the midst of struggles, it is sometimes tough to look on the bright side. Usually the silver lining is not visible until much later; but there will always be trying situations to be met, numerous lessons to be learned, and mysteries to be discovered. Often we don't know why disconcerting things occur, but if we seek for the ever-present love and blessings from God, or whatever name we have for that beautiful and meaningful source of love, we will be lifted up and shown treasures seldom found elsewhere in life.

I sincerely hope your life together as a couple and as a family will be filled with immense love, joy, happiness, and success, and that you will be able to weather even the darkest storms. Whatever time and effort you give to your partnership and your children will yield its own precious reward, and your family will call you Blessed. I wish you peace, joy, and love on your most important and exciting life journey.

There is no more lovely, friendly and charming relationship, communion, or company than a good marriage.
—Martin Luther

APPENDIX A
How Joyful Partners Treat Each Other

Marriage is a mosaic you build with your spouse.
Millions of tiny moments that create your love story.
—Jennifer Smith

I have shared a lot of ideas in the previous pages about how to maintain love and romance in your marriage. A joyful relationship is not about always being happy, contented, healthy, or without problems. Joy comes from knowing you can overcome obstacles through working together to solve any issues that come your way, even the most challenging ones. And so, all intimate relationships should be built on mutual trust, commitment, and integrity.

When challenging periods occur, you will confidently say, "I love you and want to be with you no matter what." Though a few of the following may be repetitive, here are some ideas about how to create a joyful marriage.

Joyful partners:

- Affirm how much they value each other.
- Learn the most important keys to their partner's heart.
- Implement those words and actions that are most meaningful.
- Share gratitude and appreciation.
- Are deeply committed to one another and to the promises they made.

- Are sexually faithful.
- Take responsibility for their words and actions.
- Do loving acts and speak loving words.
- Accentuate the positives rather than the negatives.
- Accept and respect one another's differences.
- Treat each other with sensitivity, respect, and compassion.
- Are friends who understand and truly "see" one another.
- Fulfill the needs of their loved one as best they can.
- Give selflessly from the heart.
- Make compromises and meet in the middle as needed.
- Resolve issues with kindness, never with retribution.
- Feel safe to ask for what they need and want.
- Nurture one another.
- Are assertive rather than aggressive, passive, or passive–aggressive.
- Negotiate to find solutions.
- Accept influence and options from one another.
- Ask for and offer forgiveness.
- Are humble, open, and sharing.
- Never cause mental or physical harm.
- Know and assert their rights and desires lovingly.
- Support and celebrate the joys and accomplishments of their partner.
- Say words and exhibit actions that earn respect.
- Encourage one another's growth and worthy endeavors.
- Grow together, finding mutual arenas in which to expand and develop.
- Learn to manage and work through problems.
- Are present, attentive, and empathetic even with stresses and struggles.

- Enjoy one another's company.
- Meet one another's emotional, physical, and sexual needs.
- Raise their children to be well-adjusted, happy, and self-reliant.
- Make time to reflect on positives, blessings, joys, and goals.
- Are abounding with love, romance, and devotion.

I know that's quite a list. Any couple who can implement all these things will have a great marriage. But it doesn't happen accidentally. Some couples do some of these things quite routinely. Others need to work at it.

My friend Jim said, "I do things for my wife because I love her. When I meet her desires, she is always more apt to meet mine." Does that seem selfish? I don't think so, because if he acts sincerely with love, she will be more likely to respond with love. Likewise, if you do things for your spouse out of love, your partner will be more likely to respond to you with love and kindness. It's a win/win process.

A successful marriage is an edifice that must be rebuilt every day.
—André Maurois

APPENDIX B
Ideas for Keeping Love and Romance Thriving

Any man who can drive safely while kissing a pretty girl is simply not giving the kiss the attention it deserves.
—Albert Einstein

I realize that all of these ideas about romantic love must take into consideration your baby, other responsibilities, and other children, if you have them. Make as many adaptations and accommodations as you can in order to implement those which resonate with you. Keep a list of the romantic actions you would like to do and those your partner would appreciate. If you haven't made your list, do it *now* and keep it readily available! It's easy to forget the great notions we once had.

Above all, don't forget that romance is first initiated in the mind and the heart. Love is the key; and then the emotion and feelings behind the actions help to create intimate and romantic moments. Any activity can be romantic, depending on how you feel toward your partner. I mean that literally—*any* activity, including labor and childbirth.

Some individuals do not like a lot of physical touch. It is important to respect that. On the other hand, negotiate and make compromises so that both of you have your needs met, at least part of the time. Give and receive physical touch with your partner if that is what is meaningful to them, even though that may not be your tendency.

And here's another reminder. Regular dates are essential, as well as spending quality time, talking, and just being together. You don't even have to leave the house or spend money if you are creative and desire to share intimate moments. Do your best to make each date special and romantic. Listen for ideas, suggestions, and requests from your spouse and do your utmost to honor them.

Here are some ideas for your list

- A loaf of bread, a jug of wine (or ginger ale), a hunk of cheese and thou, anytime, anywhere.
- Arrange for something nice to be delivered to the room if your honey is on a trip: a fruit basket, wine, chocolates, or ____.
- Ask each other for certain needs you want to be met.
- Be adventurous and mysterious. Keep some of the romance hidden to be used at just the right moment.
- Be genuinely affectionate and loving. Touch one another regularly.
- Bring home flowers or autumn leaves from the side of the road.
- Build in some time for yourself and do what you love to do.
- Buy fun surprises: lingerie, candy, flowers, or a candy bar with a love note.
- Buy gifts that have meaning.
- Clean your partner's car and spray with a nice scent.
- Continue doing sweet, unexpected acts of kindness. Men doing chores can be very romantic to a woman.
- Cook a fabulous dinner together or for the other person.

- Create a mood with candles or soft music. Implement the kind of foreplay that is most appreciated.
- Create a special dessert (or even a casserole) and hide a love message inside.
- Discuss your goals for your children and for your family.
- Do and say loving things.
- Eat out at an unusual place: a picnic table in a park, a greasy spoon, or a lovely restaurant.
- Express love and gratitude, even for the small things.
- Find a babysitter and plan a fun date.
- Find opportunities to build each other up.
- Find out what turns him/her on the most and do that.
- Fix breakfast up the canyon, on the beach, or in a meadow.
- Flirt with each other in public.
- Focus on your partner's strengths and mention them liberally.
- Give a lovely bouquet of flowers (some men love these, too).
- Give intimate hugs, squeezes, or pecks anywhere at odd moments with no expectations.
- Give spontaneous (or planned) neck and shoulder rubs, arm and hand rubs, leg and foot rubs, back rubs, or whole body massages using some nice oil or lotion. Create a mood.
- Give unexpected compliments daily.
- Go camping.
- Go for a hike or a bike ride.
- Go outside and look at the moon and the stars.
- Have a meal with candlelight on a blanket on the floor in front of the fire or by a pretty plant in the house after the baby/children are in bed.
- Hold hands under the table in a crowd of people.

- Implement the two most important keys to your partner's heart on a daily basis. (See Chapter X.)
- "Interview" and get to know each other better— your joys, dreams, favorite things, etc.
- Keep intimacy alive. Experiment with what pleases each other in the present situation.
- Kiss her ear or the back of her neck unexpectedly.
- Kiss him/her in the middle of a sentence.
- Lay out what you'd like him/her to wear for those special moments.
- Leave love notes around the house suggesting what's in store later on.
- Light a fire or lots of candles and snuggle on the floor with a blanket and soft music in the background or watch a movie.
- Listen without judgment or offering suggestions unless they are requested.
- Look lovingly at him/her.
- Mail a love letter.
- Make a special card or gift.
- Make a special meal.
- Make love in unexpected places.
- Make out in the moonlight on the porch after the kids are in bed.
- Make watching a full moon special.
- Order flowers to be delivered, or deliver them yourself.
- Pack his/her suitcase and don't say where you are going. It could just be overnight or for several days, depending on your circumstances, or even a longer trip by car, train, plane, or ship.
- Pat her cheek; hold his face in your hands as you kiss.
- Place a warm heating pad in bed for her feet during cold winter nights.
- Plan a "Celebrate My Partner Day."

- Plan a surprise getaway for a couple of hours, such as going for a drive. Look at the fall leaves, pack a picnic, and go to a park.
- Play footsie under the table.
- Play with each other's bodies sometimes and feel the excitement vs. giving in to it.
- Prepare a warm bubble bath for both of you with a lighted candle in the room.
- Pretend you don't know each other, and when you "meet," act as though you are really attracted to one another and let the drama proceed.
- Purchase some magnetic words. Create love messages and post them on the refrigerator.
- Put chocolates or surprises under his/her pillow.
- Put surprise packages together like kids do in high school when asking for a date. Ask a teen for some fun ideas.
- Read together.
- Say I love you frequently with words, looks, small actions.
- Send texts and emails that say "I love you."
- Show a strong emotional and physical desire to be close.
- Shower together.
- Sit on the couch and hold hands, or snuggle while watching movies.
- Sleep on the deck under the stars (in earshot of baby or children).
- Speak with a kind and gentle tone.
- Sprinkle rose petals on the way to the bed.
- Talk about how you fell in love and how you want to keep your relationship exciting in the future.
- Talk about your joys and dreams for the future.
- Text or email love messages.
- Watch a rainbow, crescent moon, rainclouds coming in, a sunrise, or a sunset together.

- Watch a romantic movie together while snuggling or holding hands.
- Wear flattering clothes, even when just hanging around the house.
- When stress or overwhelm set in, ask how you can help relieve the stress, and then do your best to accommodate.
- Whisper love messages and "sweet nothings" at odd moments.
- Write a love letter and hide it or mail it.
- Write love messages on the bathroom mirror with lipstick.
- Write love notes and hide them in fun places: her lingerie drawer, where he keeps his wedding ring at night, her earring box, inside a book being read, his briefcase.

These are just a few ideas. Make lists of your own. Allow your positive feelings for one another to supersede any that are negative. Remember to pick your battles. Not everything is worth a fuss. Work out your challenges, but do it in a heartful, loving way; and put some of the insignificant, unimportant matters aside in favor of your relationship.

The difference between an ordinary marriage and an extraordinary marriage is in giving just a little extra each and every day, as often as possible, for the rest of your lives.
—Unknown

Remember, the best gift you can give your children is a happy marriage!

APPENDIX C
A Few Parenting Tips

Children will not remember you for the material things you provided but for the feeling that you cherished them.
—Richard L. Evans

Many good books have been written on the subject of parenting, so you have many resources only a few steps away. Excellent classes are also available. Because I feel they are valuable, I have included here just a few concepts you may want to incorporate into your parenting. I have started with babies and progressed to toddlers and older children.

However, I want to emphasize that you should consider minimizing your ideas of being a *super parent* in favor of being a *super spouse*. Do the best you can for your children and be wonderful parents; but please focus on your marriage, as well. Without the two of you raising them together, your children will suffer.

Babies

- Breast feeding is such a lovely experience. It's so nourishing to your baby, and even a few days or weeks will provide valuable nutrients.
- Realize you each will be tired and won't get much sleep until the baby sleeps through the night. You can be angry about it or just accept the fact. Try to rest when the baby sleeps.

- Take turns rocking the baby to sleep if he is fussy and won't settle down. If Mom is up in the night more frequently, Dad can take the weekend shift so Mom can sleep in a bit. Do whatever you can to sooth him (yup, both dad and baby). Your sanity is important, so you can't "spoil" him too much at the early stage.
- Understand that life will be unpredictable, so at least for a while, try to plan things without a tight schedule.
- Babies communicate by crying, fussing, laughing, and cooing. For example, a baby will fuss if overly tired, needs a diaper change, or has a tummy ache. Learn their signals and respond as needed.
- Many parents teach their babies simple sign language before they can talk, which can take lots of stress out of figuring out what they need. You can teach them as young as six months. Use the internet and look up "sign language for babies" and enjoy the fun. I wish I had known about this.
- Show love and affection. Babies and all children need to be held, hugged, and loved. It's especially important for new babies to be held and nurtured.
- Express love verbally, use kind words, and validate often. Both parents can do this even when the baby is in the womb.
- Babies and young children need to explore their environment in order to learn. So it is important to structure your home so they are safe and in a way you won't constantly have to say "no." Certainly, they need to learn what they can do and cannot do, but if you arrange things differently for their various stages, you will be happier and so will they.
- Distraction is one of the best tools a parent can have for young children. If they are getting into

something they shouldn't, simply give them something else to do, or take them to another area.
- Go on walks with the stroller, sing, and play music. These things help brain development and will calm you as parents, too. Be involved with your child as much as you can.

A lot has been said about how to remain close during the first few weeks and months after the baby is born. Please implement the exercises and concepts, so that you will have the best chance of being a happy and joyful family.

Toddlers and Older Children

- When children are exposed to parental conflict, they may be harmed in many ways. They can exhibit low self-esteem, confusion, fear, poor school performance, emotional upset, and/or delayed development. Hostile, unresolved conflict teaches children to fight. They learn to be angry, aggressive, and controlling, and they often mimic the patterns and models they see in their parents.
- As with babies, all children need physical touch. So give hugs and kisses liberally.
- Put your children to bed as early as you can. They need sleep, and you need periods of being together alone as a couple. The housework and other chores won't go away, so talk, work out schedules and problems, and have dates at home. Do whatever you want, but enjoy things with each other.
- Ignore mild misbehaviors in your children when they are showing off, whining, having temper tantrums, sulking, begging, and so forth. Certainly, if they are being destructive or are in danger, handle the situation immediately. Kids will get attention

any way they can, so give them attention when they are behaving appropriately. This will take time to sort out.

- Be a good role model. Set a good example. Don't do things you wouldn't want others to know about. Children are blank slates and learn about the world from those close to them. They are like little sponges. Example: Don't swear in front of your kids if you don't want them to swear. Tomorrow, you just may hear them spouting off some word or words you said today.
- How about making sleeping with Mom and Dad a treat instead of a night–to–night expectation? You will have to do some gentle weaning, but it can be done.
- Take turns putting the kids to bed so they bond with both of you. Help them brush their teeth, read stories to them, etc. Develop rituals that they will remember.
- Make parenting a priority. Children grow up so fast. Remember, love is spelled TIME.
- Parents need to be joined at the hip. My advice is to support one another and get on the same page with rules, discipline, and consequences. Children learn to manipulate if they find one parent who will let them do something the other won't. This can cause confusion to a child and misery between parents. So be consistent.
- Children go through normal phases of preferring one parent over another. Each parent is the favorite at one time or another, so don't stress if you are not the chosen one. Your time will come, provided you make a concerted effort to connect with and spend time with your child.
- More than anything, we want our children to grow up to be self–confident and responsible human

beings. It starts at birth and needs to be engendered all along the way.

- Never let a child rule the moment or the day. You are the parent. The child who is constantly indulged can end up being selfish and self-centered.

- Set and keep clear boundaries. Children want them, even if they don't admit it. Teenagers really do appreciate limit setting, though they would *never, ever, ever* let you know. Boundaries actually make them feel safe and let them know they are loved. You are their protectors; so stay strong and don't allow yourself to be coerced.

- It is true that we teach people how to treat us. If you tell a child to make her bed, and when she doesn't, you make it for her, she learns, "Hey, Mom will do it, and I don't have to. Ha, ha!" So be consistent. If you make the dog stay off the couch sometimes and let him up there other times, don't be surprised if he jumps on the couch most of the time. He gets very confused. So do children.

- Follow through on your promises and commitments. If you don't do what was promised, not only do you disappoint and create upset, but you teach children to do likewise.

- Help build your child's self-esteem by empowering him to do things for himself when he is able. Have reasonable expectations. Show him how to do something, but allow him to make mistakes. Praise even small accomplishments.

- Never belittle your child (or spouse or anyone else). Use I-statements, and say what you don't like and what you would like instead. Assertiveness laced with kindness builds self-esteem. If a child acts out, counseling is a good option.

- Teach her to be responsible. Your example, plus patience and love, are needed so that she feels confident, secure, and self–assured.
- Young children love to help, so get small brooms and let them do whatever they want. They won't do it well, but let it be fun. Later on, you can teach them the right way to do things. Of course, then they won't want to so much. But give them responsibilities and help them follow through. It teaches them to be responsible. Show and tell them how to do it, and make certain there is a beginning and an end.
- As parents, you set rules, make boundaries, and dictate (in a loving way) what is okay and what is not. If your child has tantrums or is out of control and you don't know what to do, you may need help with parenting skills or developing tools for effective discipline. There are a lot of resources to draw from.
- Catch kids being good. Too often parents notice and comment on mostly the negatives. Children want attention and will try to get it by being naughty just as readily as they do by being good.
- It's easy to react harshly to our children when they do something we don't like. The time to yell is if they are going to get hurt. Be regular in setting rules and consequences when they are young, and you probably won't have to use bigger consequences when they are older.
- When parents get angry at the child, the child doesn't examine her own behavior. You take the attention off her and bring it toward you in an unwanted manner. She says to herself, "Wow, my mom is really crazy. She's losing it." Try an

experiment and see if this isn't true. Calmly ask what she did and how she plans to solve it.

- If parents have serious conflicts, children frequently act out as a means of keeping them together, because it maintains focus on the child. Kids crave attention and will get it any way they can. Minimize conflict in front of your child, but also demonstrate that you can work out disagreements.

- Speak the truth. Don't lie to your children. That doesn't mean you tell them everything; only reveal what is appropriate at the time. It's okay to say, "That is an adult issue. I will tell you when you are older." Or, "That doesn't concern you, honey." But do not lie, or they will learn to distrust you.

- If you give a child everything he wants, he will keep expecting more and will surely discover your insecurities and weaknesses. So, no spoiling. Just be clear and firm, but always do it with kindness. It isn't helpful to argue or let them beg. Provide an explanation if you think it will be helpful in the situation.

- Express love and gratitude to your children (and your spouse) for even small gestures.

- Make a plan to have regular family nights. Visit relatives, go to the zoo, have a picnic in the park, stay home and play games, work out family issues, and use these times as opportunities to teach and learn. Start when your children are young, and you will form a valuable habit that will promote family unity.

- It's nice to individually take one of your children on an outing or date once a month. It makes the child feel special and will create lasting memories. It's more challenging if you have several children, but do the best you can. Kids love one–on–one time with a caring parent.

- A happy family is about us/we, not me/I. Every day, make a close connection with each child. When my children were young, I would go to their room to tuck them into bed and ask them to tell me their "happiest experience" of the day. Often it led to important teaching moments, or they would share something they wanted to talk about.
- If you want your children to respect you, help them respect their other parent. Stand up for, defend, and protect that parent, and never let your child disparage them in any way.
- "Love and Logic" or other parenting classes are wonderful. Churches often have good classes, too.
- Develop a firm back and a soft belly. Be consistent; have rules and consequences. But at the same time, show that you love and cherish them. If you impose consequences when the issues are small, perhaps greater consequences won't be necessary when they are older. They will learn acceptable and responsible behavior while they are young, meaning you may not have huge problems later on.
- Communicate. Children need explanations, not just "because I said so." (You don't always need to explain, but do so when it is helpful.)
- Be clear with your expectations. Make it safe for them to share their feelings and talk about their lives.
- Never treat a child (or anyone) in a way you would not want to be treated.
- Give kids chores. It teaches them to be responsible. Show and tell them how to do it, and make certain there is a beginning and an end.
- They need to know it's okay to make mistakes, but they still need to learn to take responsibility. When parents admit and repair mistakes, there can be no better example.

- Teach them that mistakes and poor choices (getting a bad grade, not doing their chores, etc.) are their responsibility. You can say, "Hmm, that's too bad. What can you do about it?" Let them work it out, if they are able. If they can't, you can give them some ideas. Sometimes the consequences they come up with are better than anything you can think of. And if they don't, give them a consequence. Always leave them with a sense of dignity.

- One of the most upsetting things for parents is when siblings fight with each other. And they will. You can count on it. Teach them that there are appropriate ways to express their feelings. Help them work it out. Give them a consequence, such as, "You can continue playing together as soon as you have a plan." Some parents will have the kids hold hands or require that they look at one another for a period of time. Often they burst out laughing or just give it up.

- Teach and encourage children to send thank–you notes for gifts. Set a good example by doing so yourself.

- Aggression begets aggression, so if you are aggressive, that's what you teach your kids. Walk slowly, talk slowly, and be calm, even in the face of challenging problems. You can work out your frustrations privately. Ask lots of questions and listen to the answers.

- Children of all ages will try to manipulate you. *Do not give in!* Not even if they weep and wail, beg and holler, mock you, say they hate you, or sulk. If you are consistent and strong, coupled with gentleness but firmness, they will learn not to play you. Be especially vigilant that you and the other parent are on the same page.

- We could talk for pages and pages about mealtime. If you make too big an issue of poor eating habits, you can create eating problems for kids later in life. I recommend that you do some studying about this topic. My solution is that if they don't eat, they don't get a snack or treat until the next meal. Yes, they may be hungry, but it's a lesson they will quickly learn if they want their tummy to feel full.
- When my daughter was in third grade, she frequently forgot her lunch. I would load our baby and toddler in the car and take her lunch to school. It was a really big effort. One day I got smart and said, "Honey, if you forget your lunch, I can't bring it to you anymore. I'll try to remind you, but you can either borrow the money or just wait to eat until you get home." She didn't like borrowing money, and by the end of the day, her little tummy was growling. But she survived and didn't forget her lunch thereafter.
- Teach your children *how* to think, not *what* to think. Kids need to develop possibility thinking. "I can think for myself. I can figure things out." So give them space to do just that and don't jump to their rescue at every turn. Let them make mistakes when the cost is small. We all learn from our errors.
- Logical, natural, and realistic consequences work better than discipline. That way we empower them to be appropriately in charge of themselves—at the proper age, of course.
- If you indulge your children when they are young, allow them to control you, or teach them to be irresponsible, you can create intense problems for them and for yourself as they grow up toward adulthood and beyond.

- Help them to like and love themselves. Give sincere praise for specific things they do. If you constantly criticize them and others, they may assume they are unlovable. This can create lifelong havoc with their self–esteem.
- Above all, parents, take care of yourselves. When you take care of yourself, you will have more to give.

Parenting is hard work, but there is no more worthwhile role in the world. Each parent is different and each child is different; therefore, each family is unique. Yours is like no other, so it is necessary to learn what works for each individual within your family and situation. Since I'm sure you want to do the very best you can for your children, take advantage of the numerous books and courses that have been created. You will benefit greatly by gaining knowledge, skills, and tools that you can use for the rest of your parenting days.

If you begin sound and joyful parenting when your family is young, you will receive rich rewards by rearing self–assured, strong, independent, caring, and responsible children. And when you show love, attention, and nurturing, you will hold their hearts forever, and they will revere you always. I wish you the best in your marriage and in your parenting!

> *Our job is not to toughen our children up to face a cruel and heartless world. Our job is to raise children who will make the world a little less cruel and heartless.*
> —L. R. Knost

About the Author

Toni Erickson, MSW, LCSW
Licensed Clinical Social Worker
"The Marriage Mentor"

Before my wedding day, I dreamed of meeting a charming prince who would whisk me away to a lifetime of bliss and happiness. I did date and marry a good man, but little did I expect that after 15 years of marriage and four wonderful children, *I* would be in that dreaded category—*divorced.*

Our children were just 5, 7, 10, and 13 when my husband announced that he wanted a divorce, which was not common then. There were few useful resources that we knew of, and I honestly didn't know about counseling. I was totally devastated; life seemed not only miserable, but overwhelming for a while. Eventually my husband and I were able to work things out to make life easier for our children and for us individually, though we couldn't salvage the marriage. The kids were shattered for a time, but they turned out beautifully in spite of it all.

My own life blossomed in ways I could never have imagined. After a number of years working to support the family, as well as some not-so-good relationships, I received a Master's Degree in Social Work. It was wonderful preparation for my life, career, future dating, and eventual remarriage. How I wish I'd had the knowledge in those earlier years that I developed in school and through my life experiences. It has made me even more passionate about sharing those things with my clients, family, and others

For over 26 years, I have been happily married to a wonderful man and live in Boulder, Colorado. I finally have the love and joy I have always dreamed of. He is the man of my dreams, and I can't imagine being happier. Before we were married, we engaged in numerous discussions, exercises, and other preparations to make sure we were well suited, even though we knew we loved each other deeply. I designed most of the projects and find them very helpful for my clients today. The groundwork and roadmaps we laid are still viable and effective, and we have a very loving, close, and honest relationship.

Unfortunately, most new couples don't engage in this type of work. Having a toolbox of skills to resolve things more quickly and easily goes a long way toward facilitating joy and happiness; so does having a loving, committed, and honorable partner. I feel so very blessed to have such a wonderful partner in life.

My life and work purpose over the past 30 years has been to share my personal experience, knowledge, and skills with others to help them become happier, more deliberate, and conscious. With a place to discuss and resolve problems, to integrate skills and tools, my goal has been to make their journey of life, marriage, and child-raising easier and more fulfilling. And so I bring the words of this book to you with great joy, immense satisfaction, and heartfelt giving.

Contact Information
Book–related website and buying links:
www.dldbooks.com/tonierickson/
Personal website: www.marriage-mentor.com
Email: tonierickson.author@gmail.com
Phone: 303–579–1573

Available for couples, family, and individual coaching, speaking engagements, and workshops.

Sign up for relationship blog posts at
www.marriage-mentor.com

45116850R00165

Made in the USA
Middletown, DE
24 June 2017